THE
UNION
OF 1707

why and how?

THE UNION
OF 1707

why and how?

Paul Henderson Scott

with a special chapter on
the Equivalent by

J . G. PITTENDRIGH

THE SALTIRE SOCIETY

The Union of 1707 published 2006 by

The Saltire Society
9 Fountain Close,
22 High Street,
Edinburgh EH1 1TF

ISBN 0 85411 082 8
ISBN-13 9780854110971

Cover Design by James Hutcheson

The cover image shows a view of Queensberry House across the
roof of the Garden Lobby of the new Scottish Parliament
building. Queensberry House, now part of the Parliament, was
the home of the Duke of Queensberry who was a major player in
the events described in this book. The image is used by kind
permission of the Scottish Parliament authorities.

Printed and Bound in Scotland by Bell and Bain Limited

Contents

Other Books by Paul Henderson Scott

1707: The Union of Scotland and England Chambers 1979
Walter Scott and Scotland Saltire Society 1994
John Galt Scottish Academic Press 1985
In Bed with an Elephant Saltire Society 1985
The Thinking Nation University of Dundee 1989
Towards Independence: Essays on Scotland Polygon 1991 and 1996
Andrew Fletcher and the Treaty of Union Saltire Society 1994
Scotland in Europe: A Dialogue with a Sceptical Friend Canongate 1992
Defoe in Edinburgh and Other Papers Tuckwell Press 1995
A Mad God's Dream Edinburgh District Council 1997
Still in Bed with an Elephant Saltire Society 1998
The Boasted Advantages Saltire Society 1999
A Twentieth Century Life Argyll Publishing 2002
Scotland Resurgent Saltire Society 2003

Edited

The Age of MacDiarmid Mainstream 1980 (with A C Davis)
Sir Walter Scott's The Letters of Malachi Malagrowther Blackwoods 1981
Andrew Fletcher's United and Separate Parliaments Saltire Society 1982
A Scottish Postbag Saltire Society 1986 and 2002 (with George Bruce)
Scotland: A Concise Cultural History Mainstream 1993
Scotland's Ruine: Lockhart of Carnwath's Memoirs of the Union Association for
Scottish Literary Studies 1995 (with Daniel Szechi)
Memoirs of the Union Association for Scottish Literary Studies 1995
John Galt's The Member and The Radical Canongate 1996 (with Ian Gordon)
Scotland: An Unwon Cause Canongate 1997
The Saltoun Papers: reflections on Andrew Fletcher Saltire Society 2003
Spirits of the Age: Scottish Self Portraits Saltire Society 2005

Chapter 1

INTRODUCTION

The Union of 1707 was one of the most significant events in our history with consequences that stretched well beyond Scotland and it is also the one which is least understood. Theories about it which are contrary to the evidence have been accepted as statements of fact. Hume Brown, who wrote a *History of Scotland* early in the last century which was the standard work on the subject for many years commented on this strange state of affairs in a lecture which he gave in Oxford in 1914: "How are we to explain", he asks, "this ignorance on the part of Scotsmen generally of one of the most fateful periods in their national history?" And he suggested an explanation:

> It is a period when human nature does not appear at its best. A people does not gladly turn its eyes to a period when its representative men, whether from their own material failings or as the result of temporary circumstances, compromise the national character in the eyes of the world. So it is, perhaps, that by a kind of unconscious instinct Scotsmen have averted their gaze from a reign so momentous in their country's destinies, and abounding, moreover, in men of striking gifts and individuality".[1]

Both countries had reasons to conceal the methods by which the Union had been achieved. England had obtained their centuries long objective of asserting control over Scotland, not by conquest but by intimidation and ingenious and diverse means of bribery. They were more likely to be able to maintain it if the Union was seen as an agreed settlement and not one imposed by the larger country bullying the smaller. In Scotland the men in power were the recipients of the bribes and they therefore had every possible motive to maintain the same deception.

Curiously enough, Scottish resentment of the Union has concentrated on the bribery and not on the intimidation. "Bought and sold for English gold", as Robert Burns said. Or Walter Scott in his *Tales of a Grandfather*, a book written for children which had the frankest account of the Union that appeared anywhere in the 19th century:

> Men, of whom a majority had been bought and sold, forfeited every right to interfere in the terms which England insisted upon ...... But, despised by the English, and, detested by their own country; fettered, as Lord Belhaven expressed it, by the golden chain of equivalents, the Unionists had lost all freedom of remonstrance, and had no alternative left save that of fulfilling the unworthy bargain they had made ...... The nation, instead of regarding it as an identification of the interests of both kingdoms, considered it as a total surrender of their independence, by their false and corrupted statesmen, into the hand of their proud and powerful rival.

Scott does mention English "preparations for war on the Border which envenomed the animosity of the people of Scotland", but he does not elaborate the point. [2]

Certainly, the military threats were more discrete and less visible than the financial inducements. Perhaps also the shame of yielding to threats without a struggle was more difficult to admit. It has even been suggested that it has been responsible for inflicting lasting damage on Scottish self-confidence and self esteem.

In the course of the 19th century the Queen, the Empire and the Union (by virtue of which Scotland was a partner in it) became objects of virtually religious devotion. Even serious historians seem deliberately to have avoided criticism of any of them or any reference to any inconvenient fact. An example occurs in Hume Brown's book which I have just quoted. He prints in an appendix a letter from the Earl of Glasgow in 1711 to the English statesman Godolphin about the secret disbursement of £20,000 in 1707 to ease the passage of the Union. Hume Brown includes a sentence in which Glasgow says that if these payments had been known at the time, "the Union had certainly broken"; but without any indication that anything has been left out, he omits the phrase: "our mob and generality of Scotland being so incensed against the Union". [3]

Nineteenth century habits of reverence for the Union became so well established that the idea that it was a freely negotiated settlement became the established view. Even serious and normally scrupulous commentators quite often suggest that the Union was sought, not by England, but by Scotland for a share in the spoils of the Empire. By now, three centuries later, we ought to be able to face the reality of this event which had such important consequences.

In any case it is an extraordinary affair. Here is a Parliament, defying the wishes of its own people, voting for its own abolition and the loss of independence. In any country this would be strange and it was particularly so in a country where the conception of national independence was born in the 13th century and where it had been defended against heavy odds for more than three hundred years. It is also a fascinating if distressing story, full of surprises and unexpected twists and turns. There is very little obscurity about it, even if some episodes are puzzling, because it is well documented. Many of the participants were intelligent and articulate and many of their accounts have survived. We have the pamphlets, among others of the most effective spokesman of the opposition to the Union, Andrew Fletcher of Saltoun. One of his supporters, George Lockhart. of Carnwath, wrote the most vigorous of all Scottish political memoirs. On the other side, John Clerk of Penicuick wrote a memoir of his life, a *History of the Union* (in Latin) and two analytical essays about it. Many of the chief players both in Scotland and England reported the events in letters as they happened. From the English point of view, the most prolific writer was no less than Daniel Defoe.

It may seem surprising that the man who wrote *Robinson Crusoe, Moll Flanders* and *Roxana* should have been involved in this affair, but he became a novelist only in his sixties and his earlier career was very different. He was born in London in about 1660 to a dissenting and indeed Presbyterian family. After some unsuccessful ventures in trade he began to write for a living and indulge his taste and talent for polemics. One of his pamphlets, an attack on the Tories, offended the Government of the day and he was sentenced to be detained at the Queen's pleasure. He was eventually released by Robert Harley on the understanding that he would devote his talents to supporting the Government. In his newsletter, *The Review*, and in at least six pamphlets, all published anonymously, he supported the Union. In 1706 Harley sent him to Edinburgh as a propagandist and spy during the debate in the Scottish Parliament. He was able to ingratiate himself as a man persecuted in England because of his Presbyterianism. Afterwards he wrote a lengthy *History of the Union*.

In his propaganda Defoe indulges in the usual tricks of the trade, using different arguments for an English audience to those when he addressed the Scots. In one of the latter he professed to be a Scottish merchant living in London. His *History* is less blatantly propagandist, although it gives a false impression of the debate in the Scottish Parliament by giving the text of only two speeches,

Seton of Pitmedden for and Lord Belhaven against. There is no mention either of the arguments of Andrew Fletcher or of the repeated frustration of his own side by the Duke of Hamilton or of the influence of bribery. On the other hand on such matters as the Union of the Crowns, Darien and the English Aliens Act he reflects the Scottish rather than the English point of view and does it with his customary power and economy of language.

There is therefore plenty of material to make it possible to find answers to the obvious questions: why was there such a Union and how was it achieved? We have to begin with two events which had important consequences on subsequent developments, the Union of the Crowns and the Scottish settlement at Darien.

Chapter 2

THE UNION OF THE CROWNS, 1603

In 1503 James IV, King of Scots, married Margaret Tudor, daughter of Henry VII, King of England. The ostensible purpose was to secure peace and end the centuries of war between the two countries; but both kings knew that the marriage could lead to the succession of a Scottish king to the English throne. James may have been moved by personal ambition because there were only three lives between Margaret and her father's throne. Henry was relaxed about that possibility. A chronicler of the time tells us that some of Henry's advisors disliked the project. "They saw, just as clearly as James did, that it might bring England under the rule of a Scottish prince. Henry reassured them. If such a union took place, he argued, it would be an accession, not of England to Scotland, but of Scotland to England since the greater would always draw the less as England had drawn Normandy under her sway".[1]

The perpetual peace which was supposed to be cemented by the marriage did not last long. When Henry VIII revived the Hundred Years War against France, James IV renewed the Auld Alliance. His defeat by England at Flodden in 1513 was the most disastrous reverse ever suffered by a Scottish army. The king himself, and thousands of his subjects were killed. He had been a true renaissance prince ruling a country with an active role in European diplomacy and with high cultural achievements in architecture, in poetry with Dunbar, Henryson and Gavin Douglas and in music with Carver. Scotland survived, in Wormold's words, as "a remarkably positive, confident and successful Kingdom"; but it was a serious setback.[2]

Mary Queen of Scots, as a granddaughter of Margaret Tudor, was regarded by Catholics as the legitimate Queen of England in the place of Elizabeth. This dangerous claim led to her execution in 1587, after she had been unwise enough to put herself into Elizabeth's power. Mary's son, who became James VI, did not allow his mother's execution to weaken his ambition to inherit the English throne. Elizabeth's refusal to marry and produce an heir made James by far the strongest claimant.

For James this was a matter of personal ambition. He had been educated by the great scholar, George Buchanan, who had given intellectual substance to the Scottish doctrine that Kings were accountable to the people. James reacted against this idea and the similarly democratic views of the Scots Kirk. Andrew Melville told James that he was a member of the church, not its head and that he was only "God's sillie vassal". James, on the contrary, argued in his books, *The Trew Law of the Free Monarchies* and *Basilikon Doron*, for the "divine right of kings" and the doctrine that they were answerable to God alone. These were ideas which he could put into practice only in England where Henry VIII had prepared the way by declaring himself supreme head of Church and State. Also, Kings of England had infinitely more wealth and deference lavished on them than in the more rigorous and egalitarian atmosphere of Scotland. In succeeding to the English throne in 1603 James was accomplishing his long held ambition. As William Robertson said: "the kings of Scotland, once the most limited, became in an instant, the most absolute princes in Europe". [3]

But the Scottish people were under no illusions. They knew, like Henry VII, that this Union of the Crowns meant that it was Scotland, not England, that was being absorbed. Patrick Fraser Tytler, who wrote the first modern history of Scotland (1826-1843), based on research in the original documents, ends it with the departure of James for London because he regarded that as the end of the history of Scotland as an independent kingdom. He finishes with a melancholy passage which tells us that James as he passed the house of Seton, near Musselburgh, on his way south encountered the funeral procession of Lord Seton:

> The meeting was thought ominous by the people. It appeared, to their excited imagination, as if the moment had arrived when the aristocracy of Scotland was about to merge in that of Great Britain; as if the Scottish nobles had finished their career of national glory, and this last representative of their race had been arrested on his road to the grave, to bid farewell to the last of Scotland's kings. As the mourners moved slowly onward, the monarch himself participating in these melancholy feelings, sat down by the way-side, on a stone still pointed out to the historical pilgrim; nor did he resume his progress till the gloomy procession had completely disappeared. [4]

At the time Alexander Craig wrote a long melancholy poem, *Scotland's Tears*, to express the loss which the departure of the king had inflicted on Scotland:

> Now rivall *England* brag, for now, and not till now
> What neither wits, nor wars, not force afore could frame,
> Is now accomplisht by the death of thy Imperial Dame
> What are thou *Scotland* then? No Monarchie allace.
> A oligarchie desolate, with stay and onkow face,
> A Maymed bodie now, but shaip some monstruous thing,
> A reconfused chaos, a countrey, but a King. [5]

(but = without)

Even if he had this moment of regret, James entered into his new inheritance with vigour and enthusiasm. He made no secret of his ideas and ambitions in his speech to the House of Commons:

"The State of the monarchy is the supremest thing upon earth. For Kings are not only God's lieutenants upon earth and sit upon God's throne, but even by God Himself they are called gods".
And he urged a union between two kingdoms: "What God hath conjoined let no man separate. I am the husband and all the whole isle is my lawful wife; I am the head and it is my body; I am the shepherd and it is my flock. I hope therefore that no man will think that I, a Christian King under the gospel, should be a polygamist and husband to two wives." [6]

The House of Commons rejected the idea of a union, but James went ahead and in October 1604 assumed the title of King of Great Britain by proclamation. In spite of his inflated and often absurd language, however, James was a highly intelligent and skilful politician, with years of government in Scotland behind him. He might now, as he said, govern Scotland by a stroke of his pen, but he was more flexible than his language suggested and he surrounded himself with Scots in his court. It was his successor, Charles I, with no understanding of Scotland and without the dexterity of James, who provoked the crises in Church and State which led to the civil and religious wars. It was, as Jenny Wormold calls it, a "depressing century" [7] and for Scotland not only because of the wars, and the brief military occupation by Cromwell, but because of the effects of the Union of the Crowns.

Hume Brown said of these effects:

The Union of the crowns brought many disadvantages to Scotland, but the result of it that most vitally affected her was her severance from the nations at a period when new principles and new ideas were guiding their policy. Throughout the entire century Scotland was a severed and withered branch, and her people knew it. [8]

It is a recognition of the importance of the links between Scotland and the rest of Europe that Hume Brown should regard their severance as the most serious consequence of 1603. There were many others which were also very damaging. With the King went the control of foreign policy, the executive direction of the government, appointments to all state offices, patronage of the arts. In all these matters the King now acted on the advice of English ministers. Scottish foreign trade was sacrificed in the interest of English policy. Scotland contributed men and money to the prosecution of English wars, but was ignored in the peace settlements and was deprived of all capacity to defend herself.

The "Glorious Revolution" of 1688-9, when William and Mary replaced James VII and II, restored to the Scottish Parliament the freedom to discuss and decide as it pleased, but otherwise the royal restrictions on Scottish autonomy remained. All state appointments remained in the hands of the absentee King in London and all legislation required his assent, and that was then by no means an automatic formality as it is now.

The two Parliaments revealed their different traditions towards the institution of monarchy in their response to the change in 1688. The English Bill of Rights adopted by the English Parliament evaded the issue by asserting that James had abdicated. The Scottish Claim of Right listed abuses of powers by James and concluded that he had "invaded the fundamental constitution of the Kingdom, and altered it from a legal limited Monarchy to an arbitrary despotic power". It then declared, in the spirit of George Buchanan, that James had "forefaulted the right to the Crown".

Of course, it was not only in such points of doctrine that Scotland and England differed. The fact is, and these events cannot be understood without taking account of it, that the Scots and the English people at that time disliked and distrusted one another, an inevitable consequence of the centuries of wars between them. According to Daniel Defoe in his *History of the Union*: "Never two nations, that had so much affinity in circumstances, have had such inveteracy and aversion to one another in their blood". [9] James Anthony Froude said in his *History of England*:

> The English hated Scotland because Scotland had successfully defied them: the Scots hated England as an enemy on the watch to make them slaves. The hereditary hostility strengthened with time, and each generation added fresh injuries to the accumulation of bitterness. [10]

When James VI and I presented his proposals for a Union of Great Britain to the English House of Commons the Scots were treated with contempt.

> Hard things were said of the Scots. England was pictured as a rich pasture about to be overrun by herds of lean and hungry cattle; and Sir Christopher Piggot, almost with impunity, despite royal rage, poured forth a torrent of abuse: the Scots were proud, beggarly, quarrelsome and untrustworthy. [11]

Similar language was used in the 18th century by Wilkes and Churchill in their journal *The North Briton* and there are many examples in Boswell's account of conversations with Samuel Johnson. On 8th December 1762 Boswell reports an episode in Covent Garden when two highland officers newly returned from a campaign in the West Indies, entered a theatre:

> The mob in the upper gallery roared out: "No Scots! No Scots! Out with them!; hissed and pelted them with apples. My heart warmed to my countrymen, my Scotch blood boiled with indignation. I jumped up on the benches, roared out, "Damn you, you rascals!", hissed and was in the greatest rage . . . I hated the

English; I wished from my soul that the Union was broke and that we might give them another battle of Bannockburn. [12]

Because of such feelings as these, it is not surprising that even when the two countries had the same king after 1603 the English Parliament passed measures designed to curb Scottish competition with English trade. The most significant of these was the Navigation Act of 1651 which prohibited trade with the colonies "except in vessels owned by Englishmen or by the inhabitants of English colonies, and manned by crew of which more than one half were of English nationality". The intention evidently was to prevent Scottish participation in the colonial trade, such as tobacco from America or sugar from the West Indies. Scots did this anyway, but they were regarded by the English law as smugglers.

Daniel Defoe was frank in his *History of the Union* about the effect in Scotland of a hundred years of the joint monarchy:

> The Scots had been very sensible of the visible decay of trade, wealth and inhabitants in this country, even from the first giving away their King to the English succession; and, as the sinking condition of their nation was plainly owing to the loss of their court, concourse of people, the disadvantages of trade, and the influence the English had over their Kings; so it was as plain, there was no way to restore themselves, but either better terms of Union and alliance, or a returning back to their separate self-existing state. [13]

Chapter 3

DARIEN, 1692-1702

The 17th Century was one of steady economic decline in Scotland, because of the civil and religious wars, the Cromwellian occupation and the effect of the Union of the Crowns on Scottish trade. Because of it Scotland lost her trading privileges in France and England's wars with Holland had destroyed one of Scotland's most important markets. The English Parliament legislated to prevent Scottish participation in trade with the colonies by the Navigation Act of 1660 and the Act for the Encouragement of Trade in 1663. In addition a series of years of hot summers and early frosts did great damage to the harvests from 1695 to 1699, "the Seven Ill Years". Thousands of people died of starvation in consequence.

Clearly, drastic action was needed. Other countries in Europe, including England, had found wealth in overseas trade. Should Scotland follow that example? Andrew Fletcher addressed an aspect of the problem in his pamphlet, *The First Discourse Concerning the Affairs of Scotland* of 1698. There was now a new mercantile age. In the past, when military power had depended on unpaid feudal levies, Scotland had been able to put a force in the field which was adequate for her own defence. Now every country was obliged to defend itself by professional mercenary troops.

> But such a vast expense the riches of no country is able to support without a great trade. In this great alteration our case has been singularly bad and unfortunate: for partly through our own fault, and partly be the removal of our kings into another country, this nation, of all those who possess good ports, and lie conveniently

for trade and fishing, has been the only part of Europe which did
not apply itself to commerce; and possessing a barren country, in
less than an age we are sunk so low as to be despised by all our
neighbours and made incapable to repel an injury. [1]

In fact, Scotland's situation was even worse than this because
taxation raised in Scotland went to support the armies for
England's continental wars which were harming Scottish trade
and other interests. Scotland itself was left with almost no defence
forces at all.

The Scottish Parliament took the first step by passing an Act
which authorised Scottish merchants to form companies for
trading in all kinds of commodities in all parts of the world with
which the King was not at war. This was likely to be seen in London
as a challenge to the monopolies of the English trading companies,
but it was only an enabling Act and might not lead to further
action. William gave it his royal consent.

But there were Scots who were determined to carry out the
proposal. On 26th May 1695 the Scottish Parliament passed the
Act for a company trading to Africa and the Indies. The Company
was to have a monopoly of trade with Asia and Africa for all time
coming, and in America for 31 years. For 21 years all goods
imported by the company, except sugar and tobacco, were to be
free of duty. With the consent of the inhabitants, colonies might
be planted in any part of Asia, Africa and America, provided it was
not already in the possession on any European sovereign. In other
words, the objective was the establishment of trading posts by
agreement with the people of the country concerned, not the
establishment of colonies by military force.

William gave assent to the Act as King of Scots, but as King of
England he did all he could to frustrate it. English trading interests
and the English Parliament saw the proposal for a Company of

Scotland as a potential rival to the English East India Company. On 17th December 1695 the Lords and Commons presented an address to the King protesting against "the great prejudice, inconvenience and mischief" that would result to English trade from the Scottish Act. William replied: "I have been ill-served in Scotland, but hope some remedies may be found to prevent the inconveniences which may arise from this Act".[2]

Under the Act establishing the Company 50 per cent of the share holding was reserved to Scottish residents, and 50 per cent was available for English investors. The English share was oversubscribed within a few days, but was all withdrawn when royal displeasure was made known. English diplomatic influence in Europe discouraged continental investment. The English colonies were instructed to refuse assistance to the Scottish Company and the English Ambassador to Spain virtually encouraged a Spanish attack on the Scottish settlement.

Scotland reacted to the denial of foreign investment in the Company by a surge of patriotic fervour. All of the necessary funds were raised in Scotland alone, although it amounted to half of the total money in circulation and many people invested their entire fortune. They included members of the Scottish Parliament. English hostility had another consequence. The original intention for a Company trading to Africa, Asia and America became more problematical because even the neutrality of English colonies and navy could not be assumed. It was therefore decided to devote the entire venture to the establishment of a trading post at Darien on the Isthmus of Panama between North and South America. This had long been an aspiration of William Paterson, an ingenious Scot who among other things had proposed the foundation of the Bank of England, of which he was one of the original partners. He had the idea, 200 years before the construction of the Panama canal, that a trading settlement in the isthmus, "the door of the seas, and key of the universe" could flourish on the exchange of goods between the Atlantic and Pacific oceans.

Fletcher's *First Discourse* was published in 1698 evidently shortly after the first expedition sailed from Leith on 18th July in that year. He was clearly aware both of the prospects and the risks:

> And if it be considered, that the ships of the company are sailed; that Scotland has now a greater venture at sea than at any time since we have been a nation: that the accidents and misfortunes to which an enterprise of this nature is subject, are so many and so various, either by the loss of ships from the ordinary hazards of the sea, or hurricanes; by sickness of the men, who for the most part are neither accustomed to such long voyages, nor to climates so different from their own; by the death of one or more of those to whom the conduct of this affair is principally entrusted; by being disappointed of fresh provisions when those they carry with them are spent; by being attacked at sea or at land, before they have fortified a place for themselves, or a thousand other accidents . . . . . . Especially since the nation has so great a concern in this enterprise, that I may well say all our hopes of ever being any other than a poor and inconsiderable people are embarked with them. [3]

The expedition encountered all of these disasters, and others due to inadequate preparation and mismanagement, English hostility and Spanish attack. It ended in complete failure, abandonment of the settlement in March 1700 and the loss of most of the men and their ships. The shares in the Company in which so many Scots had invested had suddenly become worthless.

This humiliating disaster had many effects on the attitudes and on the events which followed. In Scotland it weakened the economy still further and undermined national self-confidence. The sense that the failure was at least partly due to English opposition strengthened the Scottish distrust of them. It suggested that in matters of trade, England was much more likely to resist than encourage Scottish ventures.

The first biographer of Andrew Fletcher, G.M.T. Omond, says of his reaction:

> Fletcher was a rich man, and the disaster at Darien did not mean ruin to him, as it did to so many of his countrymen. But the sight of their sufferings, the callous indifference of the English Government, and the knowledge that there was not one London merchant in a hundred who did not, in his heart, rejoice in the ruin which had befallen the Scottish traders, made him, as it made most Scotsmen, distrust England, and devote himself, heart and soul, for the rest of his life, to the cause of Scottish independence.[4]

The subsequent session of the Scottish Parliament showed that many Scots reacted in precisely the same way.

The fact that many members of the Scottish Parliament and others had lost their savings in the Darien venture presented an opportunity to the English Government to tempt Scots by offering to repay the losses if the Scottish Parliament accepted their proposals (as they eventually professed to do by the so-called Equivalent in the Treaty of Union). In England, the experience also encouraged a policy of subjecting Scotland to an even firmer control than the joint monarchy alone. That could only mean the abolition of the Scottish Parliament which had proved that it was capable of introducing measures that might offer competition to English trade. In any case, England's almost continuous war with France meant that it was, for England, a strategic necessity that

Scotland should be under firm control to avoid the risk that she might be tempted to renew her traditional alliance.

The Darien episode therefore had opposite consequences in Scotland and England. In Scotland after all the bitter experiences of the Union of the Crowns it reinforced the conviction that Scotland had to free herself from English control and assert her independence. In England it meant that Scottish independence had to be finally eradicated. English trading interests had for a century resisted any proposals for a closer association with Scotland because they were afraid that it would encourage competition from Scotland; Darien finally convinced them that they could protect their interests more effectively if Scotland was deprived of any possibility of following a policy of her own.

William and his predecessors on the combined throne of the two kingdoms needed no persuasion. It was always difficult for them to rule over two kingdoms with different attitudes, aspirations and interests. Darien had been a particularly glaring case; it involved not only a conflict between the trading interests of the two countries but the risk of a dispute with Spain with which William wanted good relations to help to curb the ambitions of France.

It has been said that the Darien episode made a Union with England more likely or even that it led directly to it. One effect was certainly to weaken the bargaining strength of Scotland and reduce her capacity to resist. On the other hand, it made any form of an amicable arrangement less likely by increasing the Scottish distrust of England.

Chapter 4

THE SCOTTISH ACT OF SECURITY, A DECLARATION OF INDEPENDENCE, 1703-4

The Darien disaster brought to a head Scottish discontent with the effects of the joint monarchy almost precisely at the time when they were presented with an opportunity to escape from it. Although Queen Anne had eighteen children, all of them died in her own lifetime, the last of them on 30th July 1700. There was no longer any obvious and automatic heir to the throne. Anne was unlikely to have more children. The legitimate line of descent from James VII and II, the Jacobite Pretender, could not be re-established without overthrowing the Protestant settlement of the "Glorious Revolution". In response to the problem, the English Parliament, without any consultation with Scotland, passed the Act of Succession of 1702. This offered the throne to Sophia, Electress of Hanover, and her descendants. Sophia had a claim to the throne because of her descent from a daughter of James VI and I; but it was only one possible solution and it was not in any way binding on Scotland.

The English Parliament and Government seem to have assumed that Scotland would merely accept their decision. This was not unusual. Although the joint monarchy began with the Scottish King James VI, his successors had become accustomed to thinking in English terms and acting on the advice of English ministers. Foreign policy and decisions about war and peace were royal prerogatives. With royal powers in London, it had become the practice for all such decisions to be taken there as if Scotland had no interest in such matters. When England declared war on

France, the ancient ally of Scotland, in 1702, for instance, Scotland was again not consulted. Since the Union of the Crowns, Scotland had no share in such matters. War was conducted in the name of England and for English interests and often against Scotland's traditional allies and trading partners. Scotland's part was confined to contributing men and money, but was forgotten again in the distribution of any benefits that might flow when peace was concluded.

The domination of England was not confined to foreign policy, but extended also to a large measure of intervention in the internal affairs of Scotland. The appointment of officers of state, that is the ministers of the Scottish Government, and all other senior appointments, were made nominally by the monarch, but again on the advice of the English Government. Money raised by taxation in Scotland was transferred to London and controlled by the English Treasury. The ministers of the Scottish Government were not only appointed, but were paid by London, and were instructed nominally by the monarch, but again in practice by the English ministers. The Scottish Parliament could debate as it pleased and pass Acts as it wished, but again they required royal assent from London. It is therefore not surprising that English Governments had become accustomed to treating Scotland as a dependency under their control.

This humiliating and damaging subordination had gradually become intolerable to all shades of Scottish opinion. There seemed now to be no reason why the Scottish Parliament could not bring the joint monarchy to an end by choosing a separate Succession to the throne. As George Ridpath wrote at the time England was already ensnared in the Succession but Scotland was still free to decide; but he expected England to resist:

> To be sure they will leave no stone unturned to drag us into it, and into all other Measures as they should think advantageous to their own Nation, though never so destructive to ours. . . . Mankind is Frail, Parliaments may be bribed and the English are both able, and never so willing to bribe as at this Juncture. [1]

Events were to prove how right he was.

At this opportune time a new Scottish Parliament was elected in 1703 and held office until it was adjourned in 1707. As with all Parliaments at that period "elected" is a term with a very restricted meaning because the electorate was only a very small part of the population. The Scottish Parliament, unlike the English, consisted of a single chamber with the Lords sitting with representatives of the burghs and the shires. The total membership was 223; of these 68 were Lords who were there by inherited right; 67 represented the burghs and were elected by the town councils which were self-perpetuating oligarchies; there were 88 members from the shires who were lairds elected by the other lairds in the same shire. That was all. There was no participation in an election at all by the general mass of population. Even so, Scottish Parliaments generally give the impression that they took their responsibilities seriously as spokesmen for the nation. They were by no means always ready to follow the lead of the senior officials appointed in the name of the monarch, the High Commissioner, the personal representative of the monarch, and the Lord High Chancellor, who presided over the debates. On the other hand the control by London over all appointments, sinecures and pensions gave the English Government a powerful means of corrupting members to adopt their policies.

In the Parliament of 1703-7 the Commissioner was the Duke of Queensberry and the Chancellor the Earl of Seafield. Commissioners were changed from year to year, but Queensberry was there at the start and again at the end; Seafield was there throughout. Both were skilful politicians and loyal servants to their masters in London. They were among the chief architects of the Union which eventually emerged from these transactions.

Parties in the modern sense of highly organised and disciplined political organisations did not then exist, but there were some recognised groups of members of similar views and aims who normally acted and voted together. Those who, for whatever reason, supported the Government were known as the Court party, led by Queensberry. The opposition was led by the Country party which claimed to represent the national interest and was led, ostensibly at least, by the Duke of Hamilton. Several times at critical moments he betrayed his own side. It was suspected at the time, and it is now clear from the surviving evidence, that he was influenced, as a contemporary delicately phrased it by "too great concern for his estate in England". [2] Andrew Fletcher of Saltoun, who had been elected to this Parliament as one of the four Commissioners for the shire of Haddington, was normally close to the Country party and he was also, for a time, supported by a group of young noblemen, known as the Squadrone Volante. Fletcher was a strong and uncorruptible advocate of independence and because of this he has been known ever since as "the Patriot". Even his political opponents respected his intelligence and integrity. The Jacobites, known as the Cavaliers, were led by the Earl of Home. They were, of course, opposed to the displacement of the Stuarts and to the Presbyterian settlement, but like the Country party they opposed English intervention in Scottish affairs.

The contemporary whom I have just quoted was a Jacobite, George Lockhart of Carnwath. He wrote an account of the proceedings of this Parliament and of subsequent events which is one of the most vivid and informative of Scottish political memoirs.

He is frank about his Jacobite feelings, but his narrative is consistent with the rest of the evidence. There are several other sources. The official record gives the text of acts, but not of speeches, apart from a few formal official statements. There was however an account of the proceedings of the 1703 session by George Ridpath which includes the text of speeches by Andrew Fletcher and they have also been printed in the collections of his writings. Unfortunately the text of his speeches in subsequent years have not survived, but it is clear from the comments in the correspondence of other members that he continued to play a prominent part for the rest of the session. I have already mentioned the writings of a leading member of the Scottish Government, Sir John Clerk of Penicuick. Several other participants wrote letters which have been published. The Earl of Mar, as Secretary of State, sent detailed reports to London. One of the members of the Parliament, Sir David Hume of Crossrig, kept a brief but useful diary of the proceedings. Gilbert Burnet was a Scot who became an English bishop, but he had been a minister of the Saltoun kirk and a tutor in the Fletcher household. He was a close observer of current affairs about which he wrote a *History of My Own Times.*

The session began on 6th May with the reading of a letter from Queen Anne. She asked the Parliament to vote supplies (a vote of money raised by taxation) for the war against France and suggested that they might consider laws to encourage trade. This was the usual tactic of the Government at the beginning of a parliamentary session in the hope that they could secure an early vote on taxation, which was all they wanted, so that the session could then be brought to an early close before any difficult questions were raised. There was no reference in any of the government statements about the real issue of the day, the Succession to the throne. Parliament was in no mood to tolerate such an evasion. On

May 19th Tweeddale for the Country party proposed an Overture that "before all other business the Parliament might proceed to make such conditions of government and regulations in the Constitution of this Kingdom to take place after the decease of Her Majestie and the heirs of her body as shall be necessary for the preservation of our religion and liberty". After several days of debate Fletcher proposed that the Overture should be put to the vote and it was passed on 28th May "by a great majority".

Already in this early stage of the session the Government had lost control. For about the next two months the debate concentrated on the disastrous consequences for Scotland of the Union of the Crowns. Fletcher did not hesitate to describe as bribes the appointment by London of such men as Queensberry and Seafield and he described the consequences:

> When our Kings succeeded to the Crown of England, the ministers of that nation took a short way to ruin us, by concurring with their inclinations to extend the prerogative in Scotland ; and the great places and pensions conferred upon Scotsmen by that court, made them to be willing instruments in the work. ...... All our affairs since the Union of the Crowns have been managed by the advice of English ministers, and the principal offices of the kingdom filled with such men, as the Court of England knew would be subservient to their designs: by which means they have had so visible an influence upon our whole administration, that we have from that time appeared to the rest of the world more like a conquered province than a free independent people. ...... Let no man say, that it cannot be proved that the English Court has ever bestowed any bribe in this country. For they bestow all offices and pensions; they bribe us, and are masters of us at our own cost. It is nothing but an English interest in this house, that those who wish well to our country, have to struggle with at this time. We may if we please,

dream of other remedies; but so long as Scotsmen must go to the English court to obtain office of trust or profits in this kingdom, those offices will always be managed with regard to the court and interest of England, though to the betraying of the interest of this nation, whenever it comes in competition with that of England. And what less can be expected, unless we resolve to expect miracles, and that greedy, ambitious, and for the most part necessitous men, involved in great debts, burdened with great families, and having great titles to support, will lay down their places, rather than comply with an English interest in obedience to the prince's commands? ..... We all know that this is the cause of our poverty, misery and dependence. But we have been for so long a time so poor, so miserable, and depending, that we have neither heart nor courage, though we want not the means, to free ourselves.[3]

Fletcher proposed a series of "Limitations" on royal powers which would have transferred them entirely to Parliament. The monarch would be obliged to sanction all laws passed by Parliament and would not have power to make peace and war or conclude treaties. "All places and offices, both civil and military and all pensions shall ever after be given by parliament". To provide Scotland with a force to defend itself, "all the fencible men of the nation, betwixt sixty and sixteen" would be armed. Any king who broke any of these conditions would be declared to have forfeited the Crown.

This was, of course, revolutionary, and outright republicanism. Even today, after 300 years of democratic progress, certain royal prerogatives remain in Britain, if in practice they are now exercised by the Prime Minister. Fletcher lost the vote, presumably because the Cavaliers, who normally supported the Country party in opposition to English interference in Scottish affairs, were not prepared to envisage so complete a removal of royal power.

But this was not a set back to the central issue. Discussion concentrated on an Act of Security, in the sense of securing Scotland against external interference. Ridpath says that four drafts were drawn up and "That which was most taken notice of, and came nearest to the Act that the House agreed to, was the Draught given in by Mr Fletcher of Saltoun". [4] The most significant sentence in the Act, was proposed by one of Fletcher's supporters, Roxburgh, on 16th July. It followed the provision for the nomination and declaration by the Parliament of a successor to Queen Anne and read:

> Providing always, that the same be not the Successor to the Crown of England, unless that in this Session of Parliament (or any other Session of this or any ensuing Parliament during her Majestie's reign) there be such conditions of government settled and enacted as may secure the honour and independency of this Crown and Kingdom, the freedom, frequency and power of the Parliament, and the religious liberty and trade of the Nation from the English or any foreign influence. [The words in brackets were added during the subsequent discussion] [5]

This was a clear declaration of independence and a firm rejection of any continuation of a joint monarchy in a form which subjected Scotland to the sort of subordination to England which she had suffered since 1603. It meant that Fletcher's limitations on the power of the monarchy would apply in the case of a joint monarchy, but not necessarily if Scotland decided a different Succession to the throne.

Two more of Fletcher's Limitations were added to the Act. The first, which had been in the preamble to the Limitations was on the cancellation of all government appointments (except for Sheriffs and Justices of Peace) on the death of the Monarch. This would allow the new parliamentary regime to start with a clean slate, free from appointments made by the Monarch under English advice. The second, in more detail than in Fletcher's original proposal, was the arming of the population, evidently to provide defence against an attack from outside. Later in the session a separate Act was passed following another of the Limitations to prevent Kings making peace and war or concluding treaties without the consent of Parliament.

When Fletcher proposed that the Act of Security should be put to the vote, Seafield adjourned the session. The House met again on 20th July when Fletcher denounced the precipitous adjournment as an illegal encroachment on the liberty of Parliament. Seafield gave an assurance, after a long discussion, that the debate would be resumed next day. The government then sprang a surprise tactic. The Lord Advocate, Stuart of Goodtrees proposed a new clause, presumably intended to take the place of Roxburgh's:

> The same person shall in no event be capable to be King or Queen of both Kingdoms of Scotland and England unless a free communication of trade, the freedom of Navigation and the liberty of the Plantations be fully agreed and established by the Parliament and Kingdom of England in favour of the subjects and kingdom of Scotland.[6]

Was this a desperate attempt by the Queensberry administration in the hope of diverting the Parliament into a course that would be less offensive to the English Government? If so, it was a bold move because he had not had time to receive fresh instructions and English Governments had always resisted any proposal to allow Scotland to participate in the colonial trade. It is possible that they had realised that freedom of trade would be a necessary consequence of an "entire union" as they in fact admitted during the talks in London in 1706 which led to the Treaty. Also both Governments probably thought that it would be a useful argument to win support in Scotland for the Union. Clerk implies this in his *Memoirs*: "it was chiefly to obtain the benefits of the plantations that the Union was agreed in Scotland, or at least it was the chief instrument used for the settlement of the question".[7] Perhaps by "chief instrument" Clerk meant the main argument, not the real reason. In his more considered view, to which I shall return later, he said that considerations about trade had little effect and that the reason for the eventual passage of the Union was the realisation that the alternative was an English invasion and the imposition of worse terms.[8]

On the other hand, it may have been an initiative by Stuart alone without consultation with his colleagues. He had the reputation of a man of independent mind. When the Union project came before the Parliament three years later, Lockhart says that he was "heartily averse" to it, and there is at least a rumour that he was behind a "protestation designed as a last ditch attempt to frustrate the Treaty." [9]

In any case, the move had no effect on Roxburgh's proposal. Parliament simply adopted both clauses. There seems to have been no great interest in a demand for freedom of trade with the English Plantations, which meant the American colonies; but there was no objection to the idea.

The whole Act, which had been approved clause by clause, was finally approved on 13th August. Hume in his diary said that it was by a majority of 59 or 60 which was substantial in a House of about 230. Fletcher said that it was:

> An act that preserves us from anarchy; an act that arms a defenceless people: an act that had cost the representatives of

this kingdom much time and labour to frame, and the nation a very great expense: an act that had passed by a great majority: and above all an act that contains a caution of the highest importance for the amendment of our constitution.

And Ridpath in his *Account of the Proceedings:*

The chief design of the Act was to secure the Nation against the pernicious Influence of a Foreign Ministry, which enslaves both our Government and People, and that it was no way design'ed to impair but support the Prerogative of the Crown of Scotland. [10]

Royal assent was not given to the Act of Security during the Session of 1703. Next year Queensberry, who had failed to secure Government business during his term of office was replaced by Tweeddale. During the next session a proposal by Roxburgh was adopted that no business should be considered before the Queen had given a response to the Act. Meanwhile Tweeddale was writing privately both to the leading English Minister, Godolphin, and to the Queen to urge approval. On 22nd July he wrote to the Queen that the Act "seems so absolutely necessary to quieten the minds of your people". He told Godolphin on the same day that the Act was the main thing Parliament insisted on "and seemed willing to accept without the clause of communication of trade". Perhaps for this reason, although it did become apparent until the Act was printed some years later, this clause was omitted from the version which received royal assent. This did not arouse comment or concern in Scotland, another indication that access to the colonial trade was not generally regarded at the time as an important issue.

The Act of Security was again read and approved on 5th August and touched with the sceptre by Tweeddale to indicate royal assent. The Scottish Parliament and the cause of Scottish independence had scored a notable victory. Years later, Daniel

Defoe said of it in his *History of the Union:*

> ... the measures taken in Scotland seemed to be well grounded,
> and their aim well taken ... This effectually Settled and Declar'd
> the Independency of Scotland, and put her in a Posture fit to be
> treated with, either by England or by any other Nation. [11]

In other words, Scotland had re-entered the community of
independent nations, in spirit at least. Ridpath in his book on the
parliamentary session of 1703 said of Fletcher's speeches that if
there was any force in "good sense, good language and strong
argument" they could not fail to explain to the country where
their true interest lay at this critical time. They gave the best
account of the Act of Security, and the Limitations and of the
"noble efforts of our Parliament to recover our ancient liberty."
Gilbert Burnet said: "A national humour of rendering themselves
a free and independent Kingdom did so inflame them, that as they
had a majority of seventy in Parliament, they seemed capable of
the must extravagant things that could be suggested to them".
And Ridpath concluded: "The memory of this Parliament will be
precious to the nation, so long as it has a being." [12]

Chapter 5

THE ENGLISH RESPONSE, 1705

It was, of course, improbable that England would now simply accept the decision of the Scottish Parliament that Scotland would reclaim her independence either by returning to a separate monarchy or by transferring all power from a joint monarch to the Scottish Parliament itself. Since the time of Edward I of England in the 13th century it had been an objective of English policy to establish control over Scotland. After centuries of futile warfare, Scotland had fallen into their hands by dynastic accident. It was not a prize that they would relinquish without a struggle.

In fact, Scotland was a prize that for England was now more valuable than ever and even indispensable. This was because of rivalry with France and the aim to become the major European and world power. In the mediaeval past Scotland as an ally of France had been a distraction, but the struggle for supremacy now made vulnerability on the northern border unacceptable. It was convenient for England to be able to draw men for her army and navy from Scotland; but the denial of Scottish territory to an enemy of England was much more important. From the English point of view, control over Scotland was now a strategic necessity.

It was also much easier to realise because the relative power of the two countries had greatly changed in favour of England, a point which Godolphin made to Seafield in a polite but menacing letter as early as 17th July 1703:

> England is now in war with France; if Scotland were in peace, and consequently at liberty to trade with France, would not that

immediately necessitate a war betwixt England and Scotland also, as has been often the case before the two nations were under the same sovereign? And though perhaps some turbulent spirits in Scotland may be desiring to have it so again, if they please to consult history they will not find the advantage of these breaches has often been on the side of Scotland; and if they will give themselves leave to consider how much England has increased in wealth and power since those times, perhaps the present conjuncture will not appear more favourable for them, but on the contrary rather furnish arguments for enforcing the necessity of a speedy union between the two nations; which is a notion that I am sorry to find has so little prevalency in the present parliament of Scotland. And I hope your lordship will not be offended with me if I take the freedom to be of opinion they may possibly be sorry for it too, when the opportunity is out of their reach. [1]

Even at this stage the threat of military intervention is unmistakable. In the course of the 17th century the economic strength of Scotland had drastically declined; and the difference in military strength was vast. Scotland had been left with virtually no defence forces at all. The English army under Marlborough was the most powerful in Europe. As T. B. Smith said in a book published in 1962:

> The Scottish commissioners in 1706 were certainly negotiating under the implied threat if negotiations failed, of invasion by one of the great captains of history at the head of a veteran army, backed by the military resources of one of the most powerful states in Europe. [2]

The military threat was therefore overwhelming, but England's financial power and especially their control over all government appointments was also a powerful weapon. Many of the classes of people who sat in Parliament or who had professional ambitions had no alternative source of income apart from such offices or sinecures. The only way to obtain an appointment in the Scottish Government was to demonstrate that you were prepared to accept instructions from London. As Fletcher said in one of his speeches in 1703 it would be miraculous if "greedy and ambitious, and for the most part necessitous men, involved in great debts, burdened with great families, and having great titles to support, were prepared to lay down their places rather than comply with an English interest in obedience to the prince's commands". [3]

Why did the Scottish Parliament accept such a humiliating and damaging condition? In view of the great disparity of military strength they had little option, but it was a procedure which reached its ultimate refinement only after the Restoration of 1660. In the earlier period during the civil wars, Scotland had much more freedom of decision. After 1660 until the "Glorious Revolution" of 1688-9, Parliaments in both countries were under rigid royal control and it was only after the revolutionary settlement that they were released from constraint. The assertion of independence by the Scottish Parliament in 1703 was virtually their first opportunity.

The English Parliament reacted to the Scottish Act of Security by passing through both Houses an "Act for the effectual securing the Kingdom of England from the apparent dangers that may arise from several acts lately passed by the Parliament of Scotland", which for brevity is usually called the Aliens Act. It was in two parts. The first provided for the authorisation of "such persons who shall be nominated by the Majesty" to "treat and consult" with Scottish Commissioners "concerning the Union of the two Kingdoms", provided that the Scottish Parliament took similar action.

In this part of the Act there was nothing that was particularly threatening either in tone or in substance. "Union" was then a vague term. The examples in the Oxford English Dictionary show that before 1707 it was used in a general sense to mean an association or alliance for any common purpose or the mere absence of dissention or discord. It was only when the English Government produced their draft of the Treaty of Union in 1706 that it acquired the meaning which is now attached to it. To make that point, it had to be described as an "incorporating Union". In 1705 there were plenty of matters on which Scotland were perfectly ready to seek an agreement with England, on trade and freedom of navigation for instance, or even to give assurances to England about the security of their northern borders.

The second part of the English Act was much more threatening in tone. Unless the Crown of Scotland had been settled in the same manner as England by 25th December 1705, from that date all Scots (except those in the forces or already settled in England) would be treated in England as aliens and incapable of inheriting property. From the same date no cattle, sheep, coal or linen (the main articles of Scottish exports) would be imported into England.

This threat of sanctions therefore applied to failure to adopt the same Succession and not to the English proposal for discussion about a Union nor to the Scottish proposal for limitations on the powers of the monarch. Presumably the English Government felt that the joint monarchy had served them so well that this is what really mattered. It is true that a joint monarch would always place restrictions on Scottish independence because of the general belief at the time that foreign policy was a royal prerogative. When James VI went south he took with him the international identity of Scotland which disappeared from the map as far as other countries were concerned. Any joint monarch would tend to have the same effect.

The Act was of doubtful legality, since Queen Anne was still Queen of both Scotland and England and the English courts had established that Scots born after 1603 could not be regarded as aliens in England. Defoe said that the Act "in a manner declar'd open war with Scotland" and that it was "the most impolitic, I had almost said unjust, that ever past that great Assembly". He added that 24 warships were fitted out to prevent the Scots trading with France and that all concerned with the general good of both Kingdoms now foresaw that war between them was unavoidable.[4] On 12th December 1704 James Johnston wrote from London to Baillie of Jerviswood: "The spirit here runs upon conquest or union".[5] As Lord Register, Johnstone was a key figure in the conduct of Scottish affairs in London and was in close touch with English official opinion.

Gilbert Burnet, said in his *History of My Own Time*:

> It was the nobility, that in every vote turned the scale for the union: they were severely reflected on by those who opposed it; it was said, many of them were bought to sell their country and their birth-right.[6]

The threats in the English Aliens Act were aimed particularly at the lords. Many of them had a financial interest through their holdings of land and exporters of the agricultural products now threatened with embargo. Also since the Union of the Crowns several lords had acquired estates in England through marriage which were at risk from the threat to ban the inheritance of property.

One of the lords with an estate in England was the Duke of Hamilton. As I have mentioned George Lockhart was afraid that he was too much concerned about it. On 15th February 1705 James Johnstone wrote from London to Jerviswood:

> Duke of Hamilton's friends are so gross as to intimate to great men here that he is chambre à louer. But for all that's to be done

now, I find its thought scarcely worth the while to make the purchase. [7]

He was wrong about he value of the purchase. As leader of the opposition in the Scottish Parliament he was a very valuable catch indeed. He demonstrated this more than once, but the most damaging to the Scottish cause was the first of his betrayals. This was during the debate on the response to the English proposal that Commissioners should be nominated for discussions about a possible union, whatever that might mean. On 1st September 1705 late in the day after a long debate after many of his supporters had left the House, Hamilton suddenly proposed that the appointment of the Scottish Commissioners should be left to the Queen. Seafield seized the opportunity and the resolution was passed. This meant of course that both the Scottish and the English teams in the discussions in London would be chosen by the English government. Any possibility of a genuine negotiation had been destroyed. The Scottish team, with only one exception, consisted of supporters of the administration appointed by the English Government in the name of the Queen, who were accustomed to acting under English instructions. The exception was a man of an entirely different disposition, George Lockhart of Carnwath, who had been included, he supposed, because he was a nephew of Lord Whartorn, a prominent English Whig.

Hamilton's action was a sudden *volte face* which took everyone by surprise. Since the 1705 session of the Parliament began on 3rd July he had repeatedly spoken in the sense of Fletcher's Limitations and the Act of Security. He had proposed or supported several measures of this kind. On 17th July, for instance, he proposed a resolution calling for limitations to secure "the liberty, religion and Independency of this Nation" and this was passed by a majority of 45.

Lockhart says of the reaction of his supporters to Hamilton's *volte-face*:

> This, you may be sure, was very surprizing to the Cavaliers and Country party; 'twas what they did not expect would have been moved that night, and never at any time from His Grace, who had, from the beginning of the Parliament to this day, roared and exclaimed against it on all occasions; and about twelve or fifteen of them ran out of the house in rage and despair, saying aloud 'twas to no purpose to stay any longer, since the Duke of Hamilton had deserted and so basely betray'd them. However, those that remained opposed it with all their might, and a hot debate arose upon it, wherein the Cavaliers used the very arguments that the Duke of Hamilton had often insisted upon this and the like occasions. [8]

Why did Hamilton, who was cheered on the streets of Edinburgh as the leader of the national cause, abandon his own supporters? Lockhart and Clerk of Penicuick both suggested that he wanted to be one of the Commissioners himself and thought that this was the best way to recommend himself to the Queen's favour.[9] But this was not the last time that he abandoned his party's cause at a crucial point. He did it again three times in the next session of Parliament. Was he deliberately playing a devious double game designed to destroy the case which he was only pretending to lead? I have already quoted some letters from the Jerviswood correspondence which shows that it was well known, or at least strangely suspected, that he was offering to sell his services to the English Government. He could presumably command a high price for such a subtle and skilful destruction of the opposition.

Hamilton was in contact with Colonel James Graham, who lived in Westmoreland and was apparently an agent of the English minister, Robert Harley. Graham reported to Harley about a conversation with Hamilton in Preston on 30th March 1705. He reports that Hamilton told him that he desired the Treaty "as much as any man in either Kingdom and will to his power promote it." He wanted "to demonstrate his services and inclinations for the Queen's services and to give undeniable proof of it ... He doth desire that from My Lord (Godolphin) or you he may be fully instructed to what point his skill or service may be required and may be plainly informed without reserve how he may be most useful". Graham then proposes a meeting between Hamilton and Harley. We do not know if this meeting took place. But there is a letter from Hamilton to Graham of 11th September 1705, a few days after his *volte-face*, which shows that he was fully conscious of the effect of his action in Parliament: "Our Parliament is now drawing to a close. I have done Her Majesty signal service in it". [10]

In fact so signal was the service which Hamilton did to the cause which was the opposite to the one he professed to lead that a modern English historian, G.M.Trevelyan, had said of the Union that Hamilton was "the instrument under Heaven of its almost miraculous passage ... So noble was his almost royal person, so high was his prestige that his followers, though they murmured at each fresh betrayal of their cause, had never the heart to renounce him in earnest". [11]

Hamilton's behaviour is astonishing, but so is the continuing loyalty of his party and of the crowds in the streets of Edinburgh. His reputation on both sides of the House was very high, until almost the end of the 1706 session. John Clerk, although on the opposite side in Parliament, said that he was "indeed a man every way fitted to be the head of a popular discontented party. He was a man of courage, and had a great deal of natural Eloquence, with much affability in his temper". Lockhart, who was one of

Hamilton's chief supporters in Parliament, uses almost the same phrase as Clerk, "never was a man so well qualified to be the head of a party" and speaks too of "his courage, of his clear, ready and penetrating conception". He could not be surprised because he always had his wits about him. Although he was cautious about entering into a new design, once he had taken it up, "nothing could either daunt or divert his zeal and forwardness".[12]

Even his own family were astonished by Hamilton's behaviour. On 10th September 1705, just nine days after his first act of treachery to his own side, his mother wrote to his sister:

> It passes my comprehension to find out a tolerable face for his actings this session of parliament and I am so ashamed on his behalfe that I know neither what to say or how to look.[13]

It seems almost incredible that anyone would be capable for two sessions of Parliament to appear both as the passionate advocate of the cause of independence and also as the man who undermined it on four decisive occasions. Perhaps he was torn between his convictions and his self-interest. Apart from the implied threat to his English estates, he had other personal interests. If Scotland decided on a separate succession he had a claim to the throne because of his Stewart ancestry. If not, his interest lay in preserving good relations with Queen Anne. In this he seems to have succeeded. After the Union, he was given a British peerage as Duke of Brandon in September 1710, and in 1712 Queen Anne appointed him as Ambassador to France and gave him the Order of the Garter. He was killed in a duel in London in the same year.

Three weeks remained before the Court, having achieved its major objective, brought the session to an end. Fletcher and the Parliament as a whole demonstrated that they had not been

demoralised by still debating and passing measures in the spirit
of the Limitations and the Act of Security. Fletcher proposed an
Act and an Address to the Queen to the effect that Scotland would
not begin talks with the English Government until the sanctions
clause of the Aliens Act had been repealed. The Address was
approved. So also was an Act for "Ministers of Scotland to be
present at foreign treaties when the Kingdom may be concerned".

Chapter 6

THE TREATY IN LONDON:
16th APRIL - 23rd JULY 1706

Modern interpretation of the questions at issue between Scotland and England in the early 18th century have been bedevilled by changes in the usage of some words. We tend to assume that union has the sense that it acquired in the Treaty of 1707, and that federation or confederation meant at that time something similar to the constitution which the United States adopted at the end of the century. In fact before these events changed their usage, the words had a completely different significance, "Treaty" in the early 18th century usually meant "negotiation", "union" was a vague term meaning any form of agreement, and "federal", according to the Oxford English Dictionary meant "of or pertaining to a covenant, compact or treaty". It was simply the adjective derived from the Latin "foedus", meaning treaty, alliance or promise. The OED describes this meaning as now obsolete, but it cites example of its use in this sense from 1660 to 1825. Confederation was used interchangeably with federation.

Thre are in fact a number of early 18th century references in Scotland which show the use of the terms union, federal or confederal as meaning an agreement by treaty which would preserve the sovereignty and Parliaments of both Scotland and England. George Ridpath, in his *Account of the Proceedings of the Parliament* tells us that the Country Party "thought no Union practicable but that of an Association, or perpetual Confederacy under the same Monarch, with an entire Reservation of the Sovereignty of each Nation and a mutual Communication of all

Privileges, which would made the Union inviolable".[1]

There is a more formal definition in a book, *The Right and Interests of the Two British Monarchies* (1703) by James Hodges, who was awarded 4800 pounds Scots by the Scottish Parliament on 31st August 1705:

> A Confederation or Federal Union is that, whereby Distinct, free and Independent Kingdoms, Dominions or States, do unite their separate Interests into one common Interest, for the mutual benefit of both, so far as relates to certain Conditions and Articles agreed upon betwixt them, retaining in the mean time their several Independencies, National Distinctions and the different Laws, Customs and Governments of each.[2]

The Earl of Mar reported that Fletcher approved of the book and thought that its arguments against an incorporating Union were unanswerable.[3]

There is very little room for doubt therefore that in Scotland in the early 18th century, when the talks proposed by the English Government were about to begin, union, federation or confederation were all terms that were generally understood to be consistent with the sovereignty and independence of Scotland and indeed as a guarantee of them. The "incorporating Union" which the English Government had in mind was the opposite, and they had to add the adjective to make that clear.[4]

One of the Scottish Commissioners was a man I have already mentioned, Sir John Clerk of Penicuick. He was a man of many talents. In his youth he had studied music in Italy and became a composer of distinction. He was interested in, and a patron of many arts, especially archaeology, painting, poetry and architecture, and he was a friend of the leading practitioners in all of these fields. As a politician, he became one of the leading members of the Scottish administration with particular responsibilities in foreign trade. His *Memoirs* are a valuable source of information about the circumstance of the Union of 1707, but in addition he wrote a *History of the Union* in Latin and two important papers about it. From these works it is clear that he admired Fletcher and respected his views, although he was on the opposite side of the House politically. He is frank in his *Memoirs* about his reaction to his appointment as a Commissioner.

> This choice, however honourable to me, was very far from giving me the least pleasure or satisfaction, for I had observed a great backwardness in the Parliament of Scotland for a union with England of any kind whatsoever, and therefor doubted not but, after a great deal of expense in attending a Treaty in England, I should be obliged to return with the uneasy reflexion of having either done nothing, or nothing to the purpose, as had been the case of former Commissioners appointed for this end. I was, in short, upon the point of refusing the Honour conferred upon me, and the rather that my father, whom I always considered as an Oracle, seldom mistaken, seemed not to approve of it. However, as at last he grew passive and that the Duke of Queensberry threatened to withdraw all friendship for me, I suffered my self to be prevailed upon, and to take journey for London with other Commissioners, and arrived there on the 13 of Aprile 1706. [5]

Almost all of the Commissioners were men who had accepted appointments by the English Government in the name of the Queen and were accustomed to acting on English instructions. Still, Clerk describes them as anxious to please the people of Scotland and to aim at a federal union, in the sense of an agreement that would preserve the Scottish Parliament and Scottish independence. He also shares a realistic assessment that the English Government would be likely to prevail and that they knew what to expect when they arrived in London. [6]

The Scottish Secretary of State, the Earl of Mar, who went to London at the end of the Parliamentary session of 1705 soon discovered that Clerk was right in his prediction. He wrote to the Earl of Cromartie on 28th November: "I find here that no Union but an incorporating relishes. I know your Lordship has long thought that the best. I wish you could persuade others of it too".[7] Cromartie was in fact one of the very few Scots at the time that we know had advocated an "entire" Union. Others were Rosebery and Stair. All three had been appointed Scottish Commissioners. On 9th March 1706 Mar wrote to Carstares in Edinburgh:

> They (the English) think all notions about foederal unions and forms a mere jest and chimera. I write this freely to you, though it is not fit this should be known in Scotland, for fear of discouraging people, and making them despair of the treaty. You see what we are to treat if is not in our choice, and that we see the inconveniences of treating an incorporating union only.

Or, as Clerk remarked, "you cannot force your will on those stronger than yourself". [8]

The negotiations, if that is the appropriate word for such an unequal confrontation, began on 16th April. The official minutes (which are printed in Vol.XI of the Acts of the Scottish Parliament) give the impression that the two delegations met face to face. From other accounts including Clerk's *History*, it appears that they met only once over the number of Scottish seats in Parliament. One of the participants, Cockburn of Ormiston, reported that they never met the English side, even to drink a glass of wine. [9]

Lockhart "had orders from his friends to sit silent and make his observations". He says that the "English cannot be blam'd for making the best bargain they could for their own country, when they found the Scots so very complaisant, as to agree to everything that was demanded of them, managing all matters in a private club". This last phrase presumably means that the real business was concluded between the leaders of the two groups before being presented for more or less automatic approval by the Commissioners as a whole.[10]

The English at the beginning tabled a proposal which summarised the whole matter:

> That the two kingdoms of England and Scotland be for ever United into one Kingdom by the name of Great Britain. That the United Kingdom of Great Britain be represented by one and the same Parliament.

They also proposed that the English Act of Succession would apply to the United Kingdom.[11]

On 24th April the Scots table an alternative proposal:

1. Succession according to the English Act.
2. Reciprocal exchange of rights and privileges between the two Kingdoms.
3. Free exchange and Intercourse of Trade and Navigation between the two Kingdoms and the Plantations.
4. All laws and statutes in either Kingdoms contrary to these terms of Union to be repealed.

This could be regarded as an attempt at a compromise. It made a substantial concession in accepting the English Succession without any safeguards of Scottish independence. In other words it ignored the Act of Security and all the subsequent legislation in the spirit of the Act and of Fletcher's Limitations which the Scottish Parliament had passed by substantial majorities during the last three years. On the other hand, it implied, in contradiction to the

English proposal, that Scotland would retain her Parliament and
still function as a separate Kingdom, but under the same monarch
as England. In other words it would be a resumption of the status
quo. It also followed the proposal for free trade with the Plantations
as in the clause suggested by the lord Advocate, Stuart of
Goodtrees, in 1703.

In fact, it was clear from their subsequent behaviour that this
was not a serious proposal for which the Scottish Commissioners
intended to put up a genuine effort. In consequence of Hamilton's
action, they were all, with the exception of George Lockhart,
supporters of the Court, men who were accustomed to acting on
instructions from London. We know from Clerk's remarks about
the preliminary discussion among the Commissioners before they
left for London that they knew in advance what the English side
were going to demand. The Scottish proposals can only have been
a faint attempt to save face, so that they could claim that they had
at least made an effort.

The English response on 24th April was a blunt refusal even to
discuss the Scottish proposal:

> (The English Commissioners) are so fully convinced that nothing
> but an entire Union of the two Kingdoms will settle perfect and
> lasting friendship between them, and they therefore think fit to
> decline entering into any further consideration of the Proposal
> now made by the Lords Commissioners of Scotland, as not
> tending to that end.

No more was said by either side about the Scottish proposal
and the discussion, or exchange of points, was confined to working
out the details of the English idea of an "entire Union", to be
defined in a Treaty of Union.

From the beginning it was clear that the English idea was that the Scottish Parliament would be abolished, but that the English one would continue as the Parliament of Great Britain with the addition of a few Scottish members. They at first proposed that Scotland should have 38 members in the House of Commons. This was the only point on which the Scots objected with some success and on which the two teams met. It was finally agreed that Scotland would have 45 members in a House of Commons of 558 and 16 Scottish Peers (out of 154) would sit in the House of Lords. This meant that the whole of Scotland would have only one more seat than Cornwall in the Commons. Burnet remarks that English bishops alone had 26 seats in the Lords compared to the total of 16 for Scotland. [12] The other Scottish lords had some compensation in the agreement that all Scottish peers would have the same privileges as English peers apart from an automatic seat in the Lords. This was of some importance to them because Scottish peers, unlike the English, had not had immunity from arrest and civil process, including debt. Since many of them were poor, this was a distinct advantage for them. There was no proposal to make any change in the number of English seats in either House.

Another major English proposal was that "the same Customs, Excises, and all other taxes, and the same Prohibitions, restrictions and regulations of Trade" would apply throughout the United Kingdom. The Scots expressed concern that the Scottish economy was not strong enough to bear the same levels of taxation as the English; but they accepted an assurance that the Parliament of Great Britain could be trusted to take care of the matter. It was agreed also that a sum of money, known as the Equivalent, would be paid to Scotland in compensation for accepting liability for a share of the English National debt. Others clauses provided for the English currency and weights and measures to be introduced into Scotland.

The Equivalent was also proposed to serve other purposes

including the repayment plus interest of investments in the Scottish Company of the Darien scheme in return for the abolition of the Company itself. Since many Scots (no doubt including members of Parliament) had invested all their available funds in the Company and thought that they had lost all of it, this was a very powerful inducement to persuade the Scottish Parliament to vote for it. But was the Equivalent, set at £398,085 10 shillings, adequate to meet all that it was supposed to cover and was in fact ever paid in full? These are questions which, curiously enough, seem never to have been adequately investigated. Not until very recently that is, when, J. G. Pittendrigh, a professional accountant of many years experience, has studied the matter in detail. I am fortunate to be able to include his report as Chapter 8 in this book.

Even if the Equivalent had been sufficient for its diverse purposes, it was not a generous English gift, but was to be repaid by charging the people of Scotland higher duties on wines, beers and spirits of which the proceeds would go to the British Treasury. Sir Walter Scott said of it:

> This large sum of money in fact belonged to the Scottish nation, being the compensation to be paid to them for undertaking to pledge their revenue for a part of the English national debt. So that, in fact, the Parliament of Scotland was bribed with the public money belonging to their own country. In this way, Scotland herself was made to pay the price given to her legislators for the sacrifice of her independence.

Lockhart was equally blunt and equally accurate. He says that the Equivalent was: "The mighty bait ... a swingeing bribe to buy off the Scots Members of Parliament from their duty to their country." [13]

But the Equivalent was not the only inducement in the Treaty. It was easy enough to dictate to the Scottish Commissioners, but the Treaty would have to be ratified by the Scottish Parliament which for the previous three years had displayed a determination to assert the independence of Scotland. So a number of measures were included designed to meet the interests precisely of the classes represented in the Parliament: for the Lords and lairds, a continuation of all heritable offices and jurisdictions; for the representatives of the burghs, all the rights and privileges of the Royal Burghs would remain entire; for the lawyers (many of whom were among the members) a whole series of measures. All Scots laws would remain in force, although alterable by the British Parliament. (It is again eloquent of the Union as a take-over and not a merger that it was not thought necessary to state that the laws of England would continue in force). The Scottish Courts would also continue in being, but subject to legislation by the British Parliament. No English Court would have the power to review or alter any sentence of the Scottish Courts. (Although it was not long before appeals were being heard by the House of Lords in London).

On 16th July the draft of the Treaty was approved and it was signed and sealed on the 22nd. Next day the Queen was presented with the document which was to take effect "if your Majesty and the Parliaments of both Kingdoms shall think fit to approve and confirm the same". In his speech on behalf of the English Commissioners the Lord Keeper William Cooper referred to the risk of war if the Union did not go through: "The great and main consequence of the Treaty" was "the continuation of peace and tranquillity in this Island . . . instead of the bloodshed and distraction which would probably follow upon the fatal division of it". Seafield, on behalf of the Scottish Commissioners, said that the Treaty was "necessary for establishing the lasting peace happiness and prosperity of both nations".

Both spokesmen were honest in these admissions that the

alternative to the Union was an English invasion. If the proposal was now accepted by the Scottish Parliament, and no opposition was to be expected in the English Commons or Lords, then England would have obtained her long-standing objective to reduce Scotland to a province. It would be achieved at very little cost and without the use of force but only by political ingenuity. England would now be able to pursue her European and world ambitions without having to worry about the security of her northern border, and with a reliable source of men and customs revenue from Scotland. As Daniel Defoe said in one of his pamphlets directed at an English audience: "It must be allow'd to say, without the least Partiality that the Advantage is wholly on England's side, whose Power is by the Addition of Scotland so fortif'd, that it must be her own Fault, if she does not make a different Figure in all the affairs of Europe, to what she ever did before".[14]

In Scotland, of course, it all looked very different. Apart from the addition of a few Scottish members to the Lords and Commons, nothing in England would be changed. The new extended Parliament could intervene in Scotland as it pleased, even in matters which the Treaty reserved to Scotland; but Scotland would be left with no constitutional means to defend her interests or views. Scottish feelings were well expressed in a letter which Robert Woodrow sent as early as 30th May 1706 to George Serle in London for George Ridpath:

I have a great many melancholy thoughts of living to See this antient Kingdome made a province, and not only our religiouse and civil liberty lost, but lost irrevocably, and that is the most dismall aspect ane incorporating union has to me, that it puts matters past help. Though many a time we have been over run and our civil and religious rights invaded, yet at the next turn we had them restored some way, as 1572, 1638, 1688. But now, once lost ever lost.[15]

Chapter 7

THE DEBATE IN THE SCOTTISH PARLIAMENT
3rd October 1706 -16th January 1707

As the first of his Limitations Fletcher proposed that there should
be annual elections for Parliament. The purpose was to reduce the
time available to the Court to work on members to win their support
by bribes, appointments, pensions and other means. The Scottish
Parliament which met on 3rd October 1706 to discuss the Treaty
drawn up in London was the same with the same membership
(apart from a few members who had died in the meantime) as the
one elected in 1703. By a majority of 60 to 80 they had resisted the
blandishments of the Court and had passed the Act of Security
and other measures in the same spirit of independence in 1703,
1704 and 1705. It was very soon apparent when they met again in
1706 that the Court and their English mentors had succeeded in
transforming the pattern of voting.

There were, of course, inducements in the Treaty itself.
Although it was a cruel deception, the Equivalent seemed to offer
repayment to the many Scots, including members of the Scottish
Parliament, who had lost their savings through the collapse of
Darien. There were the guarantees to the Scottish lawyers, the
burghs and the holders of heritable offices. There was also the
guarantee of free trade with the plantations, which English
Parliaments had always refused in the past. They presumably
regarded this as a tempting inducement, although, for reasons
which I shall discuss later, it does not seem to have had much
influence at the time in Scotland.

Then, there was the usual process of discrete bribery by one means or another. It was a normal part of the political process of patronage, but in this case it was on a much greater scale than usual because of the determination of the English Government to secure the Treaty. Burnet remarks in his *History*: "The poor noblemen and the poor boroughs made a great majority in their Parliament, and were easily to be purchased by the Court."[1] In fact this was truer of the nobles than of the burghs because unless they had large and prosperous estates they had very few means of making money except from the Government in appointments or payments of some kind.

By its nature, bribery by the simple process of handing over money was usually confidential, but in the case of the Union reliable written evidence has survived. After the Union came into effect George Lockhart became one of the Scottish members of the House of Commons. He was a member of a commission to enquire into public accounts and they uncovered correspondence about a sum of £20,000 advanced by the Queen ostensibly to defray debts of the Civil List in Scotland, but in fact to ease the ratification of the Union Treaty. The Earl of Glasgow produced a statement an oath which showed payments to members of the Scottish Parliament, ranging from £12,325 to Queensberry "for equipage and daily allowance" down to a mere £11.20 to Lord Banff.[2] "It may be doubted", Sir Walter Scott commented, "whether the descendants of the noble lords and honourable gentlemen who accepted this gratification would be more shocked at the general fact of their ancestor being corrupted, or scandalised at the paltry amount of the bribe".[3]

There is a letter in the British Museum from Glasgow and Seafield to Queensberry which confirms Lockhart's report: Godolphin, as the English Lord Treasurer, had asked Queensberry for an account of the distribution of the £20,000. Queensberry passed this request to Glasgow who had been in charge of the distribution and he replied:

May it please your Grace,
You have one accompt signed by the Earle off Glasgow, how the twenty thousand pounds advanced by my Lord Treasurer was disposed off, wee would doe anything that is in our power,to procure it to be reimbursed to his Lop. and for a considerable part of it, it may be done and stated upon the Equivalent. Your Grace's Equipage & dayly allowance will amount to betwixt twelve and thirteen thousand pounds and it is already stated as owing to your Grace, and that being a preferable debt to most off debts on the civil List, my Lord Treasurer may reckon upon it, but it is impossible for us to doe more, for what was given to the Duke of Atholl, Marquis of Tweedale, Earles off Roxburgh, Marchmont, Bellcarray, Dunmore, Cromerty and singly or evenly others in small soumes, its impossible to state these soumes without discovering this haill affair to every particular person that received any part of the money, which hath been hitherto keeped secret, and its more than probable, that they would refuse to give a signatory if they were demanded of them, so the discovering of it would be of no use, unless it were to bring discredit upon the management off that parliament; and all that will be loosed is about seven thousand pounds, if your Grace please, you may lay this befor my Lord Treasurer with that secrecy that this affair requires, wee are with all respect.

Ede 20 July 1707   May it please your Grace
                       Your Graces most faithfull & most
                       obedient humble servant
                           SEAFIELD
                           GLASGOW

Your Grace may be pleased to burn this Letter when you have read it to my Lord Treasurer. [4]

Godolphin evidently insisted on keeping the letter unburnt because it remained with his family papers until they were sold to the British Museum in 1892.

Queensberry, who was mainly responsible for carrying through the Union in Scotland, was himself well rewarded afterwards with an English Dukedom and an annual pension for life of £3,000. Even he had to be given a financial encouragement before the debate began in the Scottish Parliament. James Johnstone, who as Lord Register was closely in touch with Scottish affairs in London, wrote from there to George Baillie of Jerviswoode in code on 21st September 1706:

> Duke Queensberry, till two days before he left this, railed at the Lord Treasurer; said he was not for the Union, etc, but at last a sum of money quieted him. I believe the sum is ten thousand pounds; the thing itself is no secret. [5]

The Scottish Secretary of State, the Earl of Mar, wrote to the Duke of Argyll, who was then with Marlborough's army in Flanders, to ask him to return to Scotland to help to carry the Union. He replied on 18th July 1706:

> My Lord, it is surprising to me that my Lord Treasurer, who is a man of sense, should think of sending me up and down like a footman from one country to another without ever offering me any reward. Their is indeed a sairtin service due from every subject to his Prince, and that I shall pay the Queen as faithfully as any body can doe; but if her ministers think it for her service to imploy me any forder I doe think the proposal should be attended with an offer of a reward. [6]

A particularly interesting example of a Member of Parliament offering to sell his services is a letter from Alexander Ogilvie to Seafield in November 1704:

Pitmedden younger pretends a great keyndness to your Lo. and says most seriouslie to me that if your Lo. will obtain him a pension of one hundred pounds per annum, he will be your servant and give you a suitable returne. [7]

This refers to William Seton of Pitmedden who played an active part in the 1704 session of Parliament in support of the Country Party and Fletcher. His offer to sell his services was presumably successful because he now changed sides and wrote a pamphlet in support of the Union. In the 1706 session he made the only speech on that side of which we have the text because Defoe quotes it in his *History*. The speech turned on the issue of trade and this may have contributed to the impression that trade was the decisive issue: "This nation being poor, and without force to protect its commerce, cannot reap great advantages by it, till it partake of the trade and protection of some powerful neighbour nation, that can communicate both these". [8] Several modern historians have taken him seriously as if he were speaking and writing from conviction and not for payment.

The terms of the Treaty had been kept secret until the session of Parliament began on 3rd October 1706 because the Commissioners expected that it would provoke a hostile reaction from the people at large. They were right. Mar in one of his reports to Nairne in London on 19th November said: "I am not verie timerous and yet I tell you that every day here wee are in hazard of our lives. Wee cannot goe on the streets but wee are insulted". [9]

When Daniel Defoe wrote his *History* after the event he described the reaction of the Scottish people to the news of the Treaty in these terms:

That the figure of Scotland would make in the British Parliament would not like a Kingdom, but like a province; that one county in

England, viz Cornwall, sent up as many members, one excepted,
as the whole Kingdom; and this was an external badge of their
subjection and the like. This was a general cry, and began to be
very popular: The people cried out, they were Scotsmen and would
be Scotsmen still; they contemned the name of Britons, fit for the
Welshmen, who were made the scoff of the English, after they
had reduced them. Scotland had always had a name and fame in
foreign Courts: they were naturalised in France, enjoyed for many
years great privileges there, and honours bought with the blood
of their ancestors; and they would never give away their birthright,
though some of the nation had been driving a bargain for
themselves, at a price of selling their country. Thus they filled the
mouths of the common people, who would go about the street
crying, 'no Union', and call the treaters traitors, and soon began
to threaten them to their faces. [10]

Defoe's first reports from Edinburgh are eloquent of the
atmosphere of the time. He wrote to the English minister, Robert
Harley on 24th October. After describing how the mob attacked
the house of the former Lord provost, Pat Johnston, who had been
one of the Commissioners, he continues:

In This posture Things stood about 8 to 9 a Clock and the street
seeming passable I sallyed Out and Got to my Lodging. I had
not been Long there but I heard a Great Noise and looking Out
Saw a terrible Multitude Come up the High Street with A Drum
at the head of Them shouting and swearing And Cryeing Out all
scotland would stand together, No Union, No Union, English
Dogs and the like. I Can Not Say to you I had No Apprehensions,
nor was Monsr. De Witt quite out of my Thoughts. [11]

(De Witt was a Dutch statesman who was torn to pieces by an
infuriated mob.)

Such then was the atmosphere in Edinburgh when the
Parliament met to begin the discussion of the Treaty of Union on

3rd October 1706. Hamilton, still seen as the leader of the opposition to it because his dual role had not yet become fully apparent, was cheered wherever he appeared in the streets. Members on the Unionist side went in fear of their lives.

The first trial of strength was a vote on 15th October whether to "proceed or delay" the consideration of the Treaty. "Proceed" carried by a majority of 66. The 60 to 80 vote majority which supported the independence line in the previous three years had been reversed. All the efforts of the government during the summer to recruit support by one means or another had evidently been successful. Seafield wrote to Godolphin next day: "What occurred yesterday in Parliament gives so good hopes of success that wee thought it necessary to acquant you with it by this flying packet". [12]

He was particularly pleased by the recruitment of the Squadrone Volante, the group including Roxburgh, Tweeddale, Rothes, Baillie of Jerviswoode and others who had previously supported Hamilton and Fletcher. There is a hint in one of Mar's letters that they had been won over by a promise that they would be involved in the distribution of the Equivalent, a promise which was not kept. [13] For months the group in their letters agonised over the situation, but as early as 15th December 1705 Roxburgh wrote to Baillie: "If Union fail, war will never be avoided; and for my part the more I think of Union, the more I like it, seeing no security anywhere else". [14] He had made the same point about the danger of war on 26th December 1704: "I am thoroughly convinced that if we do not go into the Succession, or a Union, very soon, Conquest will certainly be, upon the first Peace." [13] By this he evidently meant as soon as the English armies were free from war in Europe.

For the rest of October Parliament went through the Treaty article by article without taking a vote, and then from 1st November onwards they repeated the process with a vote on each article. The

Court won all the votes, but without making much effort to reply
to the arguments of the opposition. Lockhart says that the Country
Party "took great pains to expose the unreasonableness of the
several articles as they went thro' them; but the Courtiers very
seldom made any reply, having resolv'd to trust to the number of
led-horses, and not to trouble themselves with reasoning."[15] Defoe,
probably intending it as criticism, not praise, says of the opposition:

> From article to article, they disputed every word, every clause,
> casting difficulties and doubts in the way of every argument,
> turning and twisting every question, and continually starting
> objections to gain time; and, if possible, to throw some
> insurmountable obstacle in the way.[16]

It is clear from Mar's almost daily reports to London that
Fletcher played a very active part in this determined and resolute
opposition. Defoe deals with this by making no reference in his
History of the Union to Fletcher at all, apart from his name appearing
in the voting records in an appendix. This has misled some
historians, presumably relying on Defoe as their main source, to
conclude that he had lost heart and took little part in the
proceedings. That is far from the truth.

Meanwhile, as the terms of the Treaty became known, there
was an impressive reaction from all over the country: a flood of
Addresses from shires, burghs and parishes and all social classes,
protesting against the Union as "contrary to the honour and
independency of the Kingdom". This was a remarkable and
unprecedented event which should be celebrated as a milestone
in political history. All of these Addresses, except a milder one
from Ayr, were strongly opposed to the Union and there was none
in favour. I know of no previous instance of such an unanimous,
peaceful and rational expression of the views of the people on an

important political issue. It showed the strength of national feeling and wide-spread literacy and grasp of the issues. It is especially remarkable at a time when democracy did not exist in any state and when it was widely held that people who were not landowners or Members of Parliament had no right to express views on matters of Government policy. The Addresses were read at the opening of each day's business in Parliament, but the Court paid no attention to them. Seafield said that they were only fit to make kites.

The Address from the Convention of Royal Burghs on 29th October is of particular interest, as the expression of the views of the trading community. It began with the familiar point that they were not opposed to "an honourable and safe Union with England, consisting with the being of this Kingdom and Parliaments thereof"... for they could not "expect to have the condition of the people of Scotland.... made better and improv'd without a Scots Parliament". In other words, they were in favour, like many people, of a Union in the sense of a treaty of co-operation in certain matters between the two countries which safeguarded the independence and Parliaments of both. They then described what they foresaw as the consequences of an "incorporating union" of the kind now proposed:

> And seeing by the articles of union now under the consideration of the Honourable Estates it is agreed, that Scotland and England shall be united into one kingdom, and the united kingdom be represented by one and the same Parliament, by which our monarchy is suppressed, our Parliament extinguish'd and in consequence our religion, character, claim of right, laws, liberty, trade and all that is dear to us, daily in danger of being encroach'd upon, altered or wholly subverted by the English in a British Parliament, wherein the mean representation allow'd for Scotland can never signify in securing to us the interests

reserved by us, or granted to us by the English, and by these articles our poor people are made liable to the English taxes, which is a certain insupportable burden considering that the trade is uncertain, involv'd and wholly precarious, especially when regulated as to export and import, by the laws of England, under the same prohibitions, restrictions, customs and duties: and considering that the most considerable branches of our trade are differing from those of England, and are and may be yet more discourag'd by their laws, and that all the concerns of trade and other interests are after the Union subject to such alterations as the Parliament of Great Britain shall think fit, we therefore supplicate your Grace and Honourable Estates of Parliament, and do assuredly expect that you will not conclude such an incorporating Union as is contained in the articles proposed. [17]

Even if the Court felt that it could ignore the Addresses, even from the Convention of Royal Burghs, it was much concerned about the opposition of the Kirk and its ministers. Unlike the state, the Kirk was a democratic institution with most of the people in active membership and subject to the influence of their ministers every Sunday. They had a particular reason for opposition to the Treaty in that it would subject Scotland to Government by a Parliament which overwhelmingly consisted of members of quite a different form of church and which had 26 of its bishops in the House of Lords. It is not surprising that Defoe said in one of his reports to Robert Harley that "the Rigid and Refactory Clergy" were "the worst Enemies of the Union". [18]

In an attempt to appease this resistance the Court on 6 November introduced the "Act for Security of the true Protestant Religion and Government of the Church as by law established".

This provided for the Church of Scotland as it was then constituted "to continue without any alteration to the people of this land in all succeeding generations". The Act was to be regarded as an indissoluble part of the Union and succeeding sovereigns were to subscribe and swear to it on their accession. The opposition tried to insert amendments which would make it unacceptable to the English Parliament, but it was eventually passed in its original form by 112 votes to 38.

The vote for the Church Act clearly included several of the opponents of the Union, but one of the votes on an amendment showed how firm was the control of the Court over its supporters. Hamilton at an earlier stage had drawn attention to the unfairness involved in the English Sacramental Test. If the Union came into effect, this would mean that a Scot could not hold office, or even go to a University, in England without taking an oath of allegiance to the Church of England. There would be no similar restriction on the English in Scotland. Belhaven proposed an amendment to exempt Scots from the Sacramental Test in England. Even this, which was clearly in the Scottish interest, was defeated after a strenuous debate by 39 votes.

During November and December Parliament worked systematically through the 25 articles of the Treaty, with the opposition raising many objections and moving Resolves and Protestations against it; but the Court continued to win the votes. It was clear from the divisions that the Court had won most of its support from the nobility on whom they had concentrated their efforts. Generally the votes of the nobility were about two to one for the Treaty, but both the Shires and the Burghs were firmly evenly split.

Meanwhile there were riots and demonstrations against the Treaty in Edinburgh, Glasgow, Dumfries and throughout the south and west. On 26th November Mar reported to Nairne in London that "musters and rendezvouses" were being held and that there was talk of several thousand armed men descending on Edinburgh to force Parliament to abandon the Union. He urged that as many troops as could be spared should be held in readiness in the north of England and Ireland. [19] Once again Hamilton came to the rescue of the Government. According to Lockhart, Covenanters from the south-west and Jacobites from the north agreed to make common cause and eight thousand men were ready to rendezvous in the town of Hamilton. A few days before the appointed time the Duke sent messages to call off the venture. [20]

Then towards the end of December, Atholl and Fletcher drew up a plan which Hamilton at first professed to support. This was for as many as possible of the barons, freeholders and heritors (in other words the landowners) to assemble in Edinburgh to call as a body on the High Commissioner and ask him to send a National Address to the Queen. This was to inform the Queen of "the almost universal aversion to the Treaty" and, "to prevent such a chain of miseries as is likely to be the consequence of a forced union", to ask her to discontinue the Treaty and call a new Parliament and General Assembly of the Church. Again Hamilton found a way to frustrate the opposition. He proposed to add a clause to the letter expressing willingness to accept the Hanoverian succession to the throne. Since this was repugnant to many of the landowners, an agreement could not be reached and many of them returned home, "highly enraged at being thus baulked". [21]

There was a fourth and final instance of Hamilton at first agreeing with and then frustrating the side which he professed to lead. As Parliament began the discussion of the final clauses of the Treaty in early January 1707, Hamilton himself proposed that all who were opposed to it should adhere to a protestation and a

National Address and then leave together. This document referred
to the "unprecedented number" of Addresses against the Treaty
and summarised many of the objections. It would surrender the
power of the Scottish Parliament "to the entire Parliament of
another nation" and tend to "ruin the trade and subjects of this
Kingdom, by engaging them into insupportable customs and
burdens upon foreign trade and home consumption". The
signatories declared that they refused to "lessen, dismember or
part with our Parliament, or any part of the power thereof" and
would refuse to accept "pretended laws, acts and resolves of any
pretended Parliament of Great Britain". [22]

When the day came for this firm declaration of independence,
Hamilton refused to go to Parliament with the excuse that he had
toothache. When he was eventually persuaded to go he wasted so
much time discussing who should take the lead that business
had proceeded so far that the opportunity was lost. This was the
last straw. Lockhart says that "no other measures were concerted"
and that many of the opponents of the Treaty deserted the House
in despair. [23]

In a previous chapter I discussed the mysterious conduct of
Hamilton and the equally mysterious question of why his followers
trusted him for so long. Lockhart says that on the night before this
last episode Queensberry, or someone sent by him, called on
Hamilton and warned him that if he went ahead, "England would lay
the blame upon him, and he would suffer for it". [24] This suggests that
the English Government had some hold on him, either by means of
his English estates or in some other ways; but the mystery remains.

Finally on 16th January 1707 the act ratifying the Treaty was
passed by a majority of 41. Lockhart is the source of the well-
known episode that when Seafield as Chancellor had signed the
Act, "he returned it to the Clerk, in the face of the Parliament,

with this despising and contemning remark, 'Now there's ane end of ane old sang' ". [25]

Defoe described this outcome (for which he as an English propagandist and agent had worked hard) as "contrary ... to the expectation of all the world". The Parliament of Scotland had "a long, a troublesome, a dangerous, and I must own a very uncomfortable debate, step by step, and article by article, from the third of October to the fourteenth of January, with very little intermission; for never was business closer applied, more strenuously pushed, or more vigorously opposed". He contrasted this with the smooth passage of the Treaty in the English Parliament. The debate there began in the House of Commons on 22nd January and the articles were passed one by one "without any opposition, amendment or alteration, no not in the least". It had passed through both Houses by 4th March and was approved by the Queen on the 6th. [26]

There was the same contrast between the two countries in their reactions when the Treaty came into force. Queensberry had been stoned by the crowd in Edinburgh; but, when his work as Commissioner was complete, he made a triumphal progress through England to London in April 1707. Clerk, who accompanied him, says that in all the English cities he passed through, he was received "with great pomp and solemnity; and the joyful acclamations of all the people". When he arrived at Barnet, on the outskirts of London, "he was met by the Ministry of England and most of the nobility then attending the two Houses of Parliament. Their retinue consisted of 46 coaches and above 1000 Horsemen." On May 1st, when the Treaty came into force, the Queen and both Houses of Parliament went to a service in St.Paul's "with the greatest splendour." Clerk says that he "observed a real joy and satisfaction in the Citizens of London, for they were terribly apprehensive of confusion from Scotland in case the Union had not taken place. The whole day was spent in feasting, ringing of Bells, and illuminations, and . . . at no time Scotsmen were more acceptable to the English than on that day." [27]

It was quite different in Scotland. Harie Maule wrote to Mar from Edinburgh on May 1st:

> There is nothing so much taken notice of here today as the solemnity in the south part of Britain and the want of it here. The first tune of our musick bells this day was 'Why should I be sad on my wedding day'. [28]

The different reactions in England and Scotland were significant and inevitable. For England, the Union meant the achievement of an ambition, pursued since the days of Edward I, to reduce Scotland to English domination. For Scotland, it meant the loss, in a particularly humiliating and shameful manner, of the independence which they had maintained against heavy odds for hundreds of years.

Or as Lewis Grassic Gibbon said in *Scottish Scene* in 1934:

> Everyone knew, both at home and abroad, that what really had happened was the final subjugation of the Scots by the English, and the absorption of the northern people into the name and polity of the southern. [29]

Fletcher is said to have left the final sitting of Parliament in a state of fury and with the remark that Scotland was now only fit for the slaves that had sold it. He spent most of his remaining years in Holland and France and in September 1716 died in London as he was trying to reach Saltoun before the end. His nephew who was with him at the time recorded that almost his last words were: "Lord have mercy on my poor Country that is so barbarously oppressed". [30]

Chapter 8

THE EQUIVALENT

J. G. Pittendrigh

Paul Scott in the foregoing chapters has highlighted the importance of the Equivalent as an essential element in the passing of the Treaty of Union and this has been echoed by other Scottish historians. Bruce Lenman for example writes "… it was universally agreed that without this payment there would have been no hope for the Treaty of Union." [1] However, notwithstanding the importance of this element it is difficult to find a study that follows through what actually happened to the Equivalent (Neil Munro in his very readable history of the Royal Bank of Scotland [2], now long out of print, perhaps comes closest to this) and the present chapter hopes to remedy this lack to some extent.

Firstly, it may be helpful to put the Equivalent into an English historical context by quoting from a recent work by Malcolm Balen *A Very English Deceit*. [3] This deals mainly with the history of the 'South Sea Bubble' but it also provides an interesting insight into the financial condition of England at the time:

> Many countries, but especially England and France, had empty coffers and restive taxpayers mainly because they had failed to shake off their habit of waging expensive wars against each other. Since 1688, the English government had been almost permanently in combat against the French and the Spanish. As the wars ground on, so the national debt had spiralled out of control, matched only by the harshness of the taxes on the country's landowners and the crippling generosity of the government's rate of interest to its moneylenders.

Balen goes on to say,

> In 1693 Parliament for the first time, had guaranteed the government's debt, removing the responsibility and authority for it from the monarch. The cost of borrowing money soon came to dominate political life. Within a year, in 1694, Parliament voted to establish the Bank of England as an expedient to get the government out of financial trouble. Under its charter, the Bank was required to lend more than £1million to the government, although in return it was guaranteed a profitable 8 per cent on its money. The Bank was also given permission to issue its own paper currency, and soon Exchequer bills and promissory notes were introduced to manage the debt.

As a result of the wars England's taxes were crippling. Balen notes: "More taxes are calculated to have been imposed between 1702 and 1714 than in the previous three reigns put together." This is not strictly true. What England did was to borrow money on a large scale to finance its wars although this obviously had a knock-on effect on taxes payable in later years. At the date of the Union England's National Debt was at least £14.5 million – in 1714 it had more than doubled to £36 million and 56% of British taxes were going to repay previously incurred debt (although not, as we shall see later, money owing to Scotland). [4] Thus was the debt-ridden state of the country on which Scottish unionists were pinning their hopes to bail them out of their own financial problems. England was clearly no cornucopia.

With the foregoing in mind it is now worth having a look at the crucial Article XV of the Treaty which sets forth the amount – £398,085 10 shillings – and purpose of the Equivalent. This odd-looking amount was the result of some complicated calculations by a team of six individuals, three from each side, which included William Paterson. It appeared to be the intention of the calculation to arrive at an amount to compensate the Scots for their future contribution (through taxes) towards England's debts at May 1, 1707 which clearly had not been incurred for Scotland's benefit. As mentioned above these debts were considerable and a portion of post-Union taxes raised in Scotland would be going to service them. The calculation involved all manner of estimates and assumptions and it is admitted that the figures used were imprecise. The accountancy of the day left something to be desired.[5] However, the concept behind all of this was excellent and if carried to its logical conclusion could have helped to transform Scotland's finances considerably in the post-Union years. Unfortunately, there was a built in contradiction to this arrangement as Article XV also stipulated additional uses for this money which were not included in the original calculation. One is left with the impression that the process was simply a means of putting a figure on the table which looked attractive to the Scottish negotiators. In itself £398,085 10 shillings would have sufficed to cover the losses of Darien. It would have sufficed to cover Scotland's debts. It would have sufficed to cover the costs of the recoinage. It would have certainly been sufficient to pay subsidies to the fisheries and wool industry. However, taken altogether, it was grossly deficient.

Firstly, as noted above, it was supposed to compensate the Scottish population at large for assuming a share in the English National Debt (which now became 'British'). This amounted to at least £14.5 million or about £3 a head of the English population. The Scottish debt equivalent was 5 shillings per head so by a stroke of the pen the Scots had increased their debt burden tenfold. As a temporary concession the English reduced the Scottish share of servicing this but nonetheless the capitalised value of the commitment assumed by the Scots was in fact the whole amount of the Equivalent itself. In theory the Equivalent should have been used to set up a fund to pay the Scottish contribution to the English debt over the next fifteen years or so (the period used in the calculation of the amount). Such a fund could have been of great benefit in encouraging Scottish manufactures and fisheries and in boosting the economy in general. No such fund was ever set up, hence Sir Walter Scott's assertion (quoted in Chapter 6 above) that "Scotland was made to pay the price given to her legislators for the sacrifice of her independence."

Secondly, the Equivalent was to be used to cover the costs of standardising the Scottish coinage with that of England. Money circulating in Scotland at the time consisted of a mixture of Scottish, English and continental coins of varying values many of them clipped or pared. The cost of sorting this out and reminting to the English standard came to about £50,000 or 1 shilling per head of the Scottish population. This may be the only tangible benefit that the Scots at large ever received from the Equivalent.

Thirdly, the shareholders in the African & Indian Company (involved notably, but not solely, in the Darien Scheme) were also to be compensated to the extent of £232,884 for their losses. A number of the Commissioners counted themselves among such shareholders and in one of the acts of the last Scottish Parliament the Commissioners also awarded themselves some £30,000 for 'fees and expenses' for their efforts in working so assiduously on Scotland's behalf over the years. This was also to be paid out of the Equivalent.

Lastly, any balance left over, as augmented by any increase in future Scottish revenues, was to be used for paying Scottish public debts, mainly arrears of salaries to military personnel, civil servants and so on which came to at least £160,000 and could have been as much as £250,000. [6] Much play was also made of the financial assistance to be given to Scottish manufactures and fisheries from the increase in Scottish revenues which was claimed would arise from the union under an arrangement known as 'The Arising Equivalent'. This increase, however, existed only in the imaginations of those drafting the Article. Scottish revenues in fact decreased as the union in its initial years was an economic disaster for Scotland and no such assistance was forthcoming until decades had passed and even then in trifling amounts. [7] In any event it should be noted that such assistance was to come from Scottish revenues and not from English largesse. The Scots were expected to subsidise themselves.

One does not need to be an accounting expert to detect that the Equivalent was an exercise in financial illusion. The tempting-looking amount of £398,085 10 shillings was supposed to cover liabilities and commitments, which are now seen to have totaled at least £710,000 (even ignoring the Scottish public debts of £250,000). There was a shortfall of over £300,000. In the short term the losers were mainly the public servants and their widows and orphan who were left to beg for their back pay and pensions out of the illusory 'Arising Equivalent'. [8] (Neil Munro refers to a study carried out by an official of the Royal Bank of Scotland many years ago throwing " ... the most lurid light on the shameful treatment to which for seventeen years the poorest creditors of the Union were subjected. It is a document no national historian should henceforth overlook ..." [2] Unfortunately no trace of this document can now be found.) But in the long term it was the Scottish taxpayer (and future generations of his unborn children) who was left to carry the burden of increased customs and excise charges to pay for England's past wars and this for little discernible benefit to the Scots at large. However, worse was to come.

The Equivalent was 'due and payable' from the time of the

Union and presumed to be in specie (although this was not clearly stipulated.). When the English made payment some months later it was found to amount to only £100,000 in cash. The balance was paid in what was described as Exchequer bills and notes but these could not be redeemed for cash in Scotland. This caused such uproar that a further £50,000 was later paid – but no more. Scottish creditors were left holding a pile of paper with a face value of almost £250,000 on which no interest was paid and which in practice the English would not or probably could not redeem for gold. In the five years to 1707 the English were able to mint only £82,000 worth of coinage [9] and Balen relates that in 1710 the new Chancellor of the Exchequer could only find £5,000 in the exchequer. To add insult to injury the English had borrowed money to finance the Equivalent and this was now added to the British National Debt of which the Scots had to bear their share. The Scots had helped to finance their own takeover.

The use of the £150,000 cash is not too clear. However, it is possible to deduce the following scenario. Standardisation of the coinage used up about £50,000 and there is little doubt that the Commissioners would have quickly reimbursed themselves their 'fees and expenses' of £30,000. The balance of £70,000 probably went to pay some favoured shareholders of the African & Indian Company and a few lucky creditors who had influence with the Commissioners. [10] The Darien shareholders were left with a shortfall of at least £163,000. In satisfaction of this they were forced to accept the irredeemable, non interest-bearing paper. This was now honoured with the description of 'Debentures' supposedly bearing interest at 4% or 5%. The amount of interest was academic as it was never paid and the Debentures fell rapidly in value. A Scottish Commissioner went to London at his own expense to obtain redress but was met with the "rudest and most

unmannerly things on the subject of Scotland and its claims". [2]
Interestingly he received no support from the new Scottish M.P.s
in London whose priorities lay elsewhere and returned to Scotland
empty-handed. Many desperate Darien shareholders (who had
formerly enthusiastically supported the Union) were now forced
to sell their paper to London speculators at a discount. Many (like
Paterson) were lucky to obtain 1/6th of the face value. Eventually
all but £28,000 of the Debentures ended up in London,
representing a loss of at least £170,000 to Scottish creditors (on
top of the shortfall referred to above). In 1714 new arrangements
were put in place. Interest at 5% was now to be really payable and
the Debentures were stated to be officially irredeemable. At this
stage some strange manipulations were revealed. Of the £248,000
face value of Debentures originally issued only £138,000 could be
found in circulation. Debentures of £110,000 had simply vanished
perhaps lost, destroyed or thrown away as worthless by frustrated
Scottish creditors (or their heirs as many had died in the
meantime). Back interest of £45,000 from 1708 was added to the
still circulating Debentures along with unexplained 'new claims'
of £47,000. Furthermore an amount of £18,242 was issued
specially to William Paterson to satisfy claims that he had against
the government although these had nothing to do with the original
purpose of the Equivalent. The whole added up to a sum of
£248,550 which, by coincidence or otherwise, was almost exactly
the same amount as the original issue of Debentures. From 1714
to 1719 interest payments were made on an individually authorized
basis and not as part of any regular entitlement, a system obviously
open to abuse. By this stage, as interest was now being paid, the
Debentures would have recovered some of their face value thereby
benefiting the London speculators, a number of whom must have
made tidy profits. In 1719 an annual amount of £10,000 was made

available out of Scottish revenues to pay the interest on the Debentures now mainly in English hands. The Scots, in addition to helping finance their own takeover were now funding all the interest on this. Most of this money was siphoned off to London and benefited the Scottish economy not one whit. It is interesting to note that in 1719 the Anglo-British National Debt amounted to some £42 million, almost three times the figure at the time of the union. Most of this had gone to finance new wars and to pay for previous wars. Over eighty percent of taxes raised were dissipated in this fashion. Not one penny had gone to assist Scottish manufactures or fisheries.

As a footnote to history the Equivalent Debentures were eventually redeemed in 1850. [11] From an English point of view they had effectively received a 143 years interest-free loan from the Scots of £248,000. At the end of the day England had purchased control over Scotland, its people, mineral rights, fishing and other natural assets for cash payments of only £150,000 equal to 3 shillings for every man, woman and child in Scotland at the time. At the same time they had also eliminated potential competition from the Scottish African & Indian Company. With this modest sum they had pulled off a tremendous coup for which it would be hard to find a historical parallel. In exchange the Scots received the equivalent of an 8% share in the 'British' decision-making process, the legal right to trade with the American colonies (which they had being doing in any event 'illegally') and the right of access to English markets (as, of course, the English also had to the Scots). And the Scots took on the obligation of contributing manpower and money to the many wars entered into by the Anglo-British state, including against France, The Netherlands and other countries that Scotland formerly never had any quarrel with. They also took on a share of England's debts whilst the English were absolved from any further obligation towards settling Scottish debts.

The failure of the English to honour their obligations is something that needs further investigation. Even if, in their impecunious state, they did not have enough specie to pay the balance of £248,000 owing on the Equivalent they could certainly have paid interest on their paper which would have amounted to only £13,000 per annum, a trifling sum. In 1707 the cost of servicing the English National Debt was £1,800,000 and the interest payable to the Scots was not even 1% of that. Interest must certainly have been paid to English lenders otherwise no one would have accepted the English bills that were issued in such profusion. Some may argue that exchequer bills should have had free circulation in Scotland (as had Scottish banknotes) but the Scots were not used to such a mode of payment and were understandably reluctant to adopt it. It is possible that the English were disappointed with the amount of tax revenues which were being transferred to London. Much of these were absorbed by high collection costs arising from the new bureaucracy set up as a result of the Union. Failure to pay interest was possibly a way of punishing the Scots for not yielding more revenue to the new British state. However, the debt was a 'British' one and should have been honoured accordingly.

Much of the foregoing may appear rather academic at this stage in history. However, it is not academic to reflect that how relationships start often affects the subsequent attitudes of the parties involved to each other. In 1707 the English presented themselves as the wealthy partner distributing largesse to Scotland, the poor relation. The foregoing exposition raises serious doubts as to the validity of this simple thesis. If Scotland became more prosperous many decades after the union one should consider the possibility that this may have been not *because of* but perhaps, *in spite of*, the union. In any business dealing it is elementary that one has to be careful of the other party who continually tells you what a wonderful deal you are getting whilst understating their own self-interest. A healthy questioning attitude comparing the real costs of the union to the benefits might stand Scotland in better stead than the bland acceptance of the status quo which finds such ready currency in certain quarters.

Chapter 9

WHY DID THE SCOTTISH PARLIAMENT RATIFY THE TREATY?

Why did so many members of the Scottish Parliament who had voted repeatedly for independence in 1703, 1704 and 1705 change their minds and vote to surrender it in 1706? The short answer is that they had been persuaded by a financial inducement of one kind or another; but the process of persuasion was probably more complicated than that. Many, perhaps all, of the members who changed their minds may have had a more respectable motive than financial gain alone. By 1706 they knew the terms of the Treaty and also the strength of English determination to achieve it. There were some important concessions to Scotland in the Treaty. There was little doubt that the alternative was invasion, which Scotland was in no position to resist, and the imposition of English control with no concessions at all. In these circumstances it might seem not entirely unreasonable, or dishonourable, to accept the Treaty, along with whatever private and personal inducement that might be on offer.

Some modern historians have argued that the main reason for the switch of votes to acceptance of the Treaty was the offer of free trade with the Plantations. That was certainly something to which there could be no objection; but there is little evidence that it attracted much enthusiasm in Scotland at the time. In a letter, of 25th November 1705 Roxburgh said that he thought that the Union would be accepted by the Scottish Parliament (which was obvious enough by that time) and that among the motives would be "trade with most". He did not elaborate the point, but in any case his speculations about the Treaty were endless and diverse. As I have already mentioned, he had said in an earlier letter: "If we do not go into the Succession or an Union very soon, Conquest will certainly be, upon the first Peace." [1]

It was not the possibility of trade with the Plantations which attracted attention, but the effects which the Union might have on Scotland's traditional trade in Europe. There was serious concern that the extension of English trading conditions to Scotland would greatly damage Scottish trade. As we have seen, the address from the Convention of Royal Burghs and many others made this point specifically. They were right. The immediate effect of the Union was to depress the Scottish economy for about 50 years. In his pamphlets before the Union Daniel Defoe had argued that it would make Scotland more prosperous. In his account of a tour through the country some twenty years later he admitted that the effect had been the opposite. An increase of trade and population had been "reasonably expected upon the Union" he wrote, but "this is not the case, but rather the contrary" …. "The common people all over this Country, not only are poor, but look poor, they appear dejected and discouraged." [2]

Adam Smith in a letter of 14th April 1760 said of the Union:

> The immediate effect of it was to hurt the interest of every single order of men in the country . . . Even the merchants seemed to suffer at first. The trade to the Plantations was, indeed, opened to them. But that was a trade which they knew nothing about; the trade they were acquainted with, that to France, Holland and the Baltic, was laid under new embarrassments which almost totally annihilated the two first and most important branches of it . . . No wonder if at that time all orders of men conspired in cursing a measure so hurtful to their immediate interest. [3]

Walter Scott said much the same (and remember that Walter Bagehot said of him: "You might cut paragraphs, even from his lighter writings, which would be thought acute in the Wealth of Nations". [4])

> Scotland was only tantalised by a Treaty which held out to the Kingdom the prospect of a free trade, when, at the same time, it subjected them to all the English burdens and duties, raising the expenses of commerce to a height which Scotland afforded no capital to defray so that the apprehension became general that the Scottish merchants would lose the separate trade which they now possessed, without obtaining any beneficial share in that of England. [5]

It is true of course that after Scotland (in the words of Walter Scott) had been left "under the guardianship of her own institutions to win her silent way to national wealth and consequence" [6], participation in the British Empire had profound effects on the Scottish economy. This could not have been predicted with confidence in 1706 and Parliaments are moved more by immediate effects than by distant prospects.

We have a full account of the thoughts of one of the men in the Scottish establishment who helped to bring about the Union in the writings of Sir John Clerk of Penicuick. In his youth he was under the patronage of Queensberry, who was a cousin of his first wife. After the Union he was rewarded by being made a Baron of the Scottish Court of Exchequer, an appointment which kept him in affluent ease for the rest of his life. Such matters evidently caused him no embarrassment, and he presumably regarded them as a normal part of the system. He was an honourable and intelligent man of diverse talents and interests. As I have said, Clerk was at first a reluctant unionist: but after he had committed himself to supporting Quensberry, he gave loyal service. He became a key member of the Scottish administration with particular responsibility for financial and economic matters.

There are however signs that he had an uneasy conscience for the rest of his life and felt the need to justify his conduct. After the Union he spent the next 40 years writing a history of it in Latin. In 1730 he wrote a pamphlet, *Observations on the present Circumstances of Scotland* and in 1744 a *Testamentary Memorial* for his children, brothers and friends. Both of these offered explanations of the acceptance of the Union by the Parliament. He was frank about the situation which had been created by the Union of the Crowns. In the *Observations* he says that after 1603 Scotland was "subservient to such administrators as the chief ministers in England thought fit to recommend to the Sovereign… We were in a state of absolute bondage to England." In the *History*: "Scotland's trade . . . was sacrificed to English greed" and "Scotland was left with nothing but its name and ruled like a province of England." In the *Observations* he says of Darien: "The English were so far from assisting us that they did all in their power to ruine us." There was "a moral certainty that England wou'd never allow us to grow rich and powerful in a separate state." The alternative to Union was war "and in the end the whole country would fall under the dominion of England by right of conquest… This was the principal motive both in Scotland and England for bringing about the Union." [7]

He was under no illusions about the rejection of the Union by the great majority of Scottish opinion. In the *Observations* he said that "the Articles were confirmed in the Parliament of Scotland contrary to the inclinations of at last three-fourths of the Kingdom" and in his *History* that "not even one per cent of the people approved". [8]

The English Government had made it very clear that they were simply not prepared to tolerate the restoration of Scottish independence and would resort to war if necessary. As we have seen, Godolphin did so in his letter to Seafield in 1703, and so did the English Lord Keeper when the Treaty was presented to Queen Anne in 1706. Defoe said in his *History of the Union*: "that there was no other way left, to prevent the most bloody war that ever had been between the two nations".[9]

Modern historians have drawn the obvious conclusion from the evidence. Gordon Donaldson, for instance, in 1974:

> England was not going to permit a disruption of the existing union, and the scanty and ill-trained Scottish regiments could not have resisted Marlborough's veterans.[10]

P. W. J. Riley, who made a thorough study of the evidence from the English point of view, published in 1978, comes to the same conclusion: "Contrary to an apparently reasonable hypothesis, trade considerations seem to have exerted no influence worth speaking of ... The English would not tolerate an independent Scotland". He sees "anarchy, civil war and English conquest" as the only alternative to the Union that was then available.[11]

My purpose in writing this book was to answer two questions: why was there a Union of the Scottish and English Parliaments in 1707 and how was it obtained. The answers seems to me to be very clear from the extensive evidence. Why?. Because the English Government at the time thought that they had an essential national interest in maintaining political control of Scotland. How? Because they had the skill, the means and the determination to accomplish it. They used a formidable arsenal of means: a military threat which was clear but discrete enough to avoid arousing the Scottish people; ingenious drafting of the Treaty to appeal to the self-

interest of the members of the Scottish Parliament; deception over
the Equivalent; propaganda and the use of secret agents; bribery
ranging from Dukedoms, appointments and pensions to payments
of hard cash. This was unscrupulous and deplorable; but it was
carried through with such ingenuity and persistence that it is one
of the most impressive and successful political campaigns in their
political history.

In fact it was so successful that its purpose and methods have
been largely concealed both from public opinion and even from
serious commentators down to the present. The impression has
been given, and it remains firmly embedded in public opinion,
that the Union was sought by Scotland, not by England, and that its
purpose was economic advantage. I suspect that this is the reason
(consciously or unconsciously) why many Scots still cling to it.

The English Government behaved like skilful but ruthless
confidence tricksters and many Scottish Members of Parliament
give the impression that they were too naïve to see through the
deception. On the other hand, the Addresses from the public at
large show that there was a widespread understanding of the
situation. Probably Clerk was right. Supporters of the Union in
the Scottish Parliament were probably more understanding and
sophisticated than they appeared. What was on offer was
preferable to an invasion and its consequences. So why not opt for
the lesser evil?

Another irony is that the Union did not in the end extinguish
Scotland as a nation with its own distinctive identity, attitudes
and ideas. Scottish traditions were so strong that were not easily
eradicated. Also the consequences of the Treaty in this respect
were not so harmful as they might have been, although it exerted
a strong Anglicising influence. The guarantees to the Scottish
legal system in the Treaty and to the Church in the associated

Act, along with the continuation of the Scottish systems of education and local government, for many years had more influence on Scottish attitudes than the distant British Parliament. In 1920 two distinguished historians, A. V. Dicey and R. S. Rait, one English and one Scottish and both of them enthusiasts for the Union, published a book which they had written together, *Thoughts on the Union between England and Scotland*. It reached the surprising conclusion, that the "supreme glory" of the Union was that "while creating the political unity, it kept alive the nationalism both of England and of Scotland". [12]

It was not the intention of the Treaty, but an accidental effect, that Scotland is still alive to continue to make her own distinctive contribution to civilisation. This was unintentional and it is also surprising. Especially since the introduction of broadcasting with most of it produced in London, pressure for cultural conformity with England has been intense. As the Claim of Right of 1988 said: "the Union has always been, and remains, a threat to the survival of a distinctive culture in Scotland". [13] The restoration of the Scottish Parliament in 1999 abrogated the basic provision of the Treaty of Union, although the Scottish Parliament for the time being remains under the control of Westminster. As Edwin Morgan said in his poem, *Open the Doors*, for the opening of the new Scottish Parliament building in October 2004:

> When you convene you will be reconvening,
> With a sense of not wholly the power,
> Not yet wholly the power,
> But a good sense of what was once in the honour of your grasp.

So far, it is only a beginning, but Scotland has already been restored to the international community to an extent that had been denied to it since 1603.

REFERENCES

Abbreviation		Source
Burnet		Gilbert Burnet, *History of His Own Times* (Oxford 1823) 6 vols.
Clerk	Memoirs	*Memoirs of the Life of Sir John Clerk of Penicuick* Ed. John M Gray (SHS, Edinburgh 1892)
	History	*History of the Union of Scotland and England* Ed. By Douglas Duncan (SHS, Edinburgh, 1993)
	Observations	*Observations on the present Circumstances of Scotland, 1730* Ed. T. C. Smout in Vol.X, of *Miscellany of the Scottish History Society* (Edinburgh 1965) pp 174-212
	Testamentary Material	Printed as Appendix C in *History* (above)
Defoe	History	*The History of the Union between England and Scotland* (London, 1786)
	Letters	*The letters of Daniel Defoe* Ed. G.H.Healey (Oxford 1969)
Fletcher	Letters	*Letters of Andrew Fletcher of Saltoun and his family 1715-16* Ed. Irene J. Murray, in Vol.X *Miscellany*. (Scottish History Society, 1965) pp 143-173
	Writings	*Fletcher of Saltoun, Selected Writings* Ed. David Daiches (ASLS, Edinburgh 1979)

Jerviswood	*Correspondence of George Baillie of Jerviswood* (Bannantyne Club, 1842)
Lockhart	*The Lockhart Papers*, ed. Anthony Aufere (London, 817) 2 volumes. There is a recent edition of his *Memoirs of the Union: Scotland's Ruine*, ed Daniel Szechi with a foreword by Paul Scott. (ASLS, Aberdeen, 1995)
Mar	Report of the Manuscripts of the Earl of Mar and Kellie (Historical Manuscripts Commission, London 1904)
Ridpath	*An account of the Proceedings of the Parliament of Scotland which met at Edinburgh, May 6 1703* (Edinburgh 1704)
Seafield	*Letters relating to Scotland in the Reign of Queen Anne by James Ogilvy, First Earl of Seafield and others* Ed. by P.Hume Brown (Edinburgh 1915)

Chapter Notes

1. INTRODUCTION

1 Hume Brown, *The Legislative Union of England and Scotland* (Ford Lectures, Oxford 1914)

2 Sir Walter Scott, *Tales of a Grandfather* (edition of 1899), pp. 770;754

3 As 1 above: the full text of the letter is in H.M.C. MMS of Duke of Portland, Vol.V (London 1899) pp.114-5

2. THE UNION OF THE CROWNS, 1603

1 Polydore Vergil, *Historia Anglica*, Vol.II pp.1539-40 Quoted by R.L.Mackie in *King James IV of Scotland* (Edinburgh, 1988) p.91

2 Jenny Wormold, *Scotland: A History* (Oxford, 2005) p. xx

3 William Robertson, *History of Scotland* (20th Edition, London 1817) Vol.III, p.192

4 Patrick Fraser Tytler, *The History of Scotland*, (Edition of 1864) Vol.IV, p.316

5 Alexander Craig, in *Scotland's Poets and the Nation*, ed. by Douglas Gifford and Alan Riach (Manchester, 2004) pp. 45-6

6 Quoted in D.H.Willson, *King James VI and I* (London, 1956) pp. 243, 251

7 As 2 above, p.xviii

8 Hume Brown, *The Union of 1707* (Glasgow, 1907) p.4

9 Defoe, *History*, p.37

10 James Anthony Froude, *History of England* (London, 1873) Vol.IV p.5

11 As 6 above, p.255

12 James Boswell, *London Journal*, 1762-1763 (London, 1950) pp. 21-2

13 Defoe, *History*, p.74

3. DARIEN, 1692-1702

1 Fletcher, *Writings*, p.31

2 Hume Brown, *History of Scotland* (Cambridge, 1909) Vol.III, p.30

3 Fletcher, *Writings*, p.30

4 G. M. T. Omond, *Fletcher of Saltoun*, (Edinburgh, 1897) p.48

4. THE SCOTTISH ACT OF SECURITY, 1703-04

1 Ridpath, p.304

2 Lockhart, Vol.I, p.56

3 Fletcher, *Writings*, pp.70-72

4 Ridpath. p.132

5 *Acts of Parliament of Scotland*, Vol.XI pp.136-7

6 As 5 above: Vol.XI p.69

7 Clerk, *Memoirs*, pp. 53-4

8 Clerk, *Observations*, p.191

9 Lockhart, Vol.I, p.207

10 Fletcher, Writings, p.85, Ridpath, p.271

11 Defoe, *History*, p.52-3

12 Burnet, Vol.V, p.98; Ridpath, pp. 174-5

5. THE ENGLISH RESPONSE, 1705

1   HMC Report XIV Appendix Part III, p.198   Text also in J.M.Graham: *Annals and Correspondence of the Viscount and 1ˢᵗ and 2ⁿᵈ Earls of Stair* (1875) Vol.I pp. 380-381

2   T.B.Smith, "The Union of 1707 as Fundamental Law" in *Studies Critical and Comparative* (Edinburgh, 1962) p.9

3   Fletcher, *Writings*, p.71

4   Defoe, *History*, pp. 86 and 54

5   Jerviswood, p.42

6   Burnet, Vol.V. p.181

7   Jerviswood, p.42

8   Lockhart, Vol.I, p.132

9   Lockhart, Vol.I, p.136, Clark, *Memoirs*, p.57

10 H.M.C. 10th Report, App.IV (1885) p.340

11 G. M. Trevelyan, *England Under Queen Anne* (London 1932), Vol.II pp.224-5

12 Clerk, *Memoirs*, p.57; Lockhart, Vol.I pp.55-6

13 Atholl MS 45 V1 120; quoted by Rosalind R. Marshall in her entry on James Hamilton, 4ᵗʰ Duke of Hamilton in ODNB

6. THE TREATY IN LONDON

1   Ridpath, p.332

2   James Hodges, Op.Cit. (London, 1703) p.3

3   Mar, p.267

4   Scottish Record Office Misc.260/1 (Fletcher to Russell 8/1/1689). Quoted by T. C. Smout in his essay "The Road to Union" in *Britain After the Glorious Revolution* edited by Geoffry Holms (London, 1969) pp.183-4

5 Clerk, *Memoirs*, p.58

6 Clerk, *Memoirs*, p.60

7 Mar, p.289

8 *State papers and Letters Addressed to William Carstares*, edited by Joseph McCormick (Edinburgh 1794) pp 743-4; Clerk, *History*, p.162

9 Mar, p.271

10 Lockhart, Vol.I, pp. 156-7

11 APS, Vol.XI, Appendix p.165

12 Burnet, Vol.V, pp. 224; 286

13 Sir Waler Scott, *Tales of a Grandfather*, edition of 1889, p.769; Lockhart, Vol.I, pp. 156-7

14 Defoe, in his pamphlet, *At Removing National Prejidicis Against A Union with Scotland*, (London, 1706) p.26

15 *Early Letters of Robert Woodrow* (1698-1709) ed.L.W.Sharp (Edinburgh, SHS 1937) p.291

7. THE DEBATE IN THE SCOTTISH PARLIAMENT

1 Burnet, Vol.V, p.292

2 Lockhart, Vol.I, pp.262-268

3 Sir Water Scott, *Tales of a Grandfather* (Edition of 1889), p.769

4 British Museum, Add.MSS 34, 180

5 Jerviswood, p.160

6 Mar, p.270

7 *Correspondence of James, Fourth Earl of Findlater and First Earl of Seafield, and James Grant* (Edinburgh HS, 1912) p.382

8 Defoe, *History*, pp. 312-16

9 Mar, p.329

10   Defoe, *History*, p.226

11   Defoe, *Letters*, p.135

12   Seafield, p.96

13   Jerviswood, p.141

14   Jerviswood, p.28

15   Lockhart, Vol.I, p.162

16   Defoe, *History*, p.254

17   Lockhart, Vol.,I p.171-3

18   Defoe, *Letters*, p. 226

19   Mar, p.335

20   Lockhart, Vol.I pp. 196-201

21   Lockhart. Vol.I pp.. 203-205

22   Lockhart, Vol.I pp. 207-211

23   Lockhart, Vol.I p. 214

24   Lockhart, Vol.I pp. 212-214

25   Lockhart, Vol.I, p. 223

26   Defoe, *History*, pp. 475 and 484-485

27   Clerk, *Memoirs*, pp. 67-69

28   Mar, p.389

29   Lewis Grassic Gibbon, *Scottish Scene* (London 1934) p.35

30   *Letters of Andrew Fletcher of Saltoun and his Family* ed. by Irene J. Murray (SHS, Miscellany X, Edinburgh 1965) p.171

8. THE EQUIVALENT

1   Bruce Lenman in *The Jacobite Rising in Britain 1689-1746* (London 1980) p.86

2   Neil Munro *History of the Royal Bank of Scotland 1727-1927* Edinburgh 1928 p.21 et seq.

3   Malcolm Balen, *A Very English Deceit* London 2002 pp. 14-15

4   Mitchell / Deane *Abstract of British Historical Statistics* (Cambridge 1971). These and other figures quoted later on in the chapter are taken from the section on Public Finance pp. 386-401

5   P.W.J. Riley *The English Ministers and Scotland 1707-1727* (London 1964) p. 204 et seq. Riley notes that the Equivalent involved "some ponderous working out". He refers to a purchase period of 15 years 3 months but gives no discount rate and from the information given it is not possible to check the computation. However, by working backwards one finds that £398,085 is the capitalised value of £38,350 payable over 15 years three months discounted at 5% which is a reasonable assumption. Presumably something in the region of this amount was the expected Scottish contribution to the British Exchequer towards England's pre-Union debts. In Henry Hamilton's *An Economic History of Scotland in the Eighteenth Century* (Oxford 1963) Appendix III shows excise revenues alone to be in excess of this amount for the period concerned so England presumably got its money's worth.

6   P.W.J. Riley *The Union of England and Scotland* (Manchester 1978) p.336. Riley's figure appears to be the best documented of all the estimates used by various historians

7   The BBC Scottish History website notes: "the economic impact of free trade with England was disastrous for over 30 years" ... and Scottish revenues in fact diminished. This is little wonder as a substantial portion had arisen from customs on English goods imported into Scotland – and such customs dues were

no longer levied. Moreover goods formerly imported directly into Scotland from the Continent now went via England which pocketed the relative customs revenues.

8 A number of efforts appear to have been made in the post-Union period to show that the "Arising Equivalent" actually arose. For example, the writer has seen in the Scottish Records Office in Edinburgh (Ref. GD18/2699) a semi-illegible handwritten document dated 1712 and headed "Account of the Equivalent which now appeared due by England to Scotland according to the 15th article of the Treaty of Union". This purports to shows a calculation of the growth of excise for the five years to 1712. However, there is no indication that these efforts were crowned with any degree of success.

9 Mitchell / Deane, ibid p. 439

10 J.S. Shaw, *Political History of 18th Century Scotland* (Edinburgh 1999) Chapter 1, "The Price of Scotland", contains a great deal of research on this matter showing that supporters of the Union appear to have been rather favoured in the distributions.

11 These debentures had meantime (through The Equivalent Company in 1727) been instrumental in the foundation of the Royal Bank of Scotland – but that is another story.

9. WHY DID THE SCOTTISH PARLIAMENT RATIFY THE TREATY?

1 Jarviswood, pp. 138 and 28

2 Daniel Defoe, *A Tour Thro' the Whole Island of Great Britain* (London 1727), Vol.III, pp. 33 and 69

3 Adam Smith, *Correspondence*, ed by E.C.Mosner and I.C.Ross (Glasgow, 1994), p.68

4 Walter Bagehot, *Collected Works* (London, 1995) pp.416-419

5 Sir Walter Scott, *Tales of a Grandfather* (Edinburgh 1889) p.733

6   Sir Walter Scott, *The Letters of Malachi Malagrowther* (Edition of 1981, Edinburgh) p.10

7   Clerk, *History*,pp. 79,81,191,192

8   Clerk, *Observations*, p.192, *History*, p.118

9   Defoe, *History*, p.64

10 Gordon Donaldson, *Scotland: the Shaping of a Nation* (Newton Abbot and London, 1974) p.57

11 P. W. J. Riley, *The Union of England and Scotland* (Manchester, 1978) pp. 281;177-8; 314

12 A.V.Dicey and R.S.Rait *Thoughts on the Union Between England and Scotland* (London 1920) p.362

13 *Claim of Right*, Text in a book of that title, ed. Owen Dudley Edwards, (Edinburgh 1989) para 2.2

Other Saltire Books by Paul H Scott

Walter Scott and Scotland

This stimulating introduction to Sir Walter Scott throws new light on both the great man himself and on the dilemma which faced Scotland at the time and which faces it still. It is a succinct and penetrating account of the influences on Scott of both classical and enlightened Edinburgh, and of border and Jacobite traditions.

ISBN 0 85411 056 9   Price £7.99

Still in Bed with an Elephant

A study of Scotland's relations with England which is, of course, the elephant in question. As well as a cultural history in the period since the Union of 1707, the book offers individual studies of leading observers such as Sir Walter Scott, Robert Burns, Andrew Fletcher of Saltoun and Sir John Clerk of Penicuik. The author identifies the distinctive contribution made by Scottish culture to world civilisation and at the same time helps remove some myths and misunderstandings. He makes a the case for independence as part of a world-wide need to conserve individuality and diversity.

ISBN 0 85411 073 9   Price £7.99

The Boasted Advantages

In this new work Paul Scott attempts to answer Robert Burns' question posed in 1790: 'what are the boasted advantages which my country reaps from a certain union?' Scott examines the often advanced theories that the union was a bargain over trade and that it brought, and indeed continues to bring, great advantages to Scotland. In so doing he helps sweep away the fog of myth and propaganda allowing a rational judgement about the course of Scotland's post union history and the best road to follow in the future.

ISBN 0 85411 072 0   Price £6.99

Andrew Fletcher and the Treaty of Union

Andrew Fletcher has been known since his own lifetime as 'The Patriot' because of his determined resistance to the parliamentary Union of Scotland and England in 1707. This book, the first on Fletcher since 1953, combines a biography with a full account of the events leading to the Union and an up-to-date analysis of Fletcher's essays and speeches.

"impeccably researched and convincing ... will remain the definitive study for many years."   Michael Lynch in *The Scotsman*

ISBN 0 85411 057 7   Price £12.99

The Saltoun Papers: Reflections on Andrew Fletcher

Since the 1960s Andrew Fletcher has been commemorated each September by a short lecture in East Saltoun Parish Church where he is buried. Over the years some of the country's most distinguished historians, politicians and writers have offered their thoughts on Fletcher, and on Scotland past and present. In *The Saltoun Papers* fifteen of these talks selected from the years 1979 to 1999 are reproduced, including those by historians Gordon Donaldson, Geoffrey Barrow, Bruce Lenman, William Ferguson, David Simpson, Edward Cowan and Murray Pittock, politicians Neil MacCormick and John Hume Robertson, philosopher Alexander Broadie, writers Arnold Kemp, Billy Kay and Sheila Douglas, and the businessman, Sir Iain Noble. Paul Scott, the distinguished historian and writer on Fletcher and his period, edited the papers and his own address at East Saltoun in 1984 is included.

A wide range of topics is covered: identity, nationalism, language, patriotism, the Union of 1707 in all its manifestations, and relations with Europe and the world, and controversial and often opposing views are argued with passion and authority.

ISBN 0 85411 081 X Price £9.99